THE CATHOLIC PERSPECTIVE ON PAUL

PAUL AND THE ORIGINS OF CATHOLIC CHRISTIANITY

TAYLOR R. MARSHALL

ORIGINS OF CATHOLIC CHRISTIANITY TRILOGY
VOLUME TWO

SAINT JOHN PRESS
MMX

Sacred Scripture citations generally from the 1899 edition of the Douay-Rheims (Challoner) Bible, or based upon it.

Marshall, Taylor
The Catholic Perspective on Paul:
Paul and Origins of Catholic Christianity / Taylor Marshall
2nd Edition April 23, 2021
Includes bibliographical references and index
ISBN: 978-0-578-05016-4
1. Paul 2. New Testament. 3. Theology. I. Title.

Published by
Saint John Press
PO Box 568011
Dallas, Texas 75365

Printed in the United States of America
Acid-free paper for permanence and durability
Covert Art: Steven M. Nelson {smnelsondesign.com}

Dedicated to my lovely wife Joy with whom I share a "great sacrament" (Eph 5:32 Douay-Rheims).

After these events, Paul resolved in the Spirit to pass through Macedonia and Achaia and go to Jerusalem, saying, "After I have been there, **I must also see Rome"** (Acts 19:21).

The following night the Lord stood by Paul and said, "Take courage, for just as you have testified about me at Jerusalem, **so you must also bear witness at Rome"** (Acts 23:11).

I rejoice in my sufferings for your sake, and in my flesh **I complete what is lacking in Christ's afflictions for the sake of His Body, that is, the Church"** (Col 1:24).

CONTENTS

ACKNOWLEDGEMENTS

As a schoolchild who seeks to honor his mother with a drawing, I place this book into the loving and fragrant hands of my **Blessed Mother Mary**. May she in turn, present it to our **Lord Jesus Christ** to the greater glory of **God the Father.** If any word of this book is false, prideful, pompous, incorrect, or contrary to the doctrine of the Holy Catholic Church, may it be rejected and attributed to my ignorance. If there be anything of worth and goodness, may it be attributed to the divine Mercy of God.

O ALTITUDO DIVITIARUM SAPIENTIÆ, et scientiæ Dei: quam incomprehensibilia sunt judicia ejus, et investigabiles viæ ejus! Quis enim cognovit sensum Domini? aut quis consiliarius ejus fuit? aut quis prior dedit illi, et retribuetur ei? Quoniam ex ipso, et per ipsum, et in ipso sunt omnia: ipsi gloria in sæcula. Amen.

How I Discovered the Catholic Paul

My first prayer came as a response to reading the words of Saint Paul. I did not grow up in a Christian home; however, when I was about nine years old, my father presented me with the autograph of the catcher for the Texas Rangers, Darrel Porter, who had written under his signature "Rom 10:9." Thinking it to be a secret code, I quickly cracked it after discovering it to be the abbreviation of a Bible verse. When I looked up the verse, I read these inspired words from the pen of Saint Paul:

> For if thou confess with thy mouth the Lord Jesus, and believe in thy heart that God hath raised him up from the dead, thou shalt be saved (Rom 10:9).

In that moment, I prayed my first prayer, "I believe that You raised Jesus from the dead," and I confessed with my mouth that "Jesus is the Lord." Thereafter, I began to read the Bible in order to learn more about my Lord who had risen from dead. God works in mysterious ways...even through baseball. The Spirit breatheth where he will.

About nine years later, the summer after I graduated from high school, my mother took us on a vacation to Italy. We flew into the airport outside of Rome and our taxi driver drove us into the marvelous city—the Eternal City. I could not believe my eyes as we wound through the city. I saw the story of civilization flash before me—thousands of years of history and the most magnificent buildings that I had ever seen. As Saint Francis once remarked, "Blessed is he who expecteth nothing, for he shall enjoy everything."

As a generic Christian without denominational commitments, I was completely unaware of the five hundred year debate between Catholics and Protestants. I knew that I was not a "Catholic," but I didn't know why. I began exploring Rome as an alien in a foreign land. Here and there I discovered details about the amazing superstitions of Catholics. I say "amazing superstitions" because they truly amazed me. I was not yet a hardened Protestant and hardly felt the need to "protest" against Rome at all. However, I was generally suspicious of the gold ceiling in Saint Peter's Basilica. Nevertheless, I thought to myself, "If anyone deserves a gold ceiling, it would be God." The marble churches piqued my interest as I came into contact with a form of Christianity that did not conform to my experience.

Although the form of religion confused me, I saw Scriptural events depicted everywhere in the sacred art of Rome. I also saw depictions of holy virgins, bloody martyrs, and popes—people completely foreign to me—yet sewn seamlessly into the fabric of biblical themes. For example, I remember a tour guide showing us the Altar of St. Leo the Great carved by Alessandro Algardi. The monumental marble relief depicts Pope Leo I († A.D. 461) repelling Attila the Hun and his armies from Rome. I asked the tour guide, "Who are those men in the sky—the two men flying like superheroes and bearing swords?"

"Ah yes," replied the guide, "those two men are the Apostles Peter and Paul, the founders of the Church of Rome."

I certainly knew who Peter and Paul were from the Bible, and I had been aware that they came to Rome (after all, the book of Acts ends with Paul in Rome—more on that later). However, I was somewhat confused by the fact that Catholics believed that Peter and Paul (two men now in heaven) were still somehow interested in Rome. I was even more perplexed by the belief that Peter and Paul would appear centuries after their deaths in the sky with swords raised high against heathen invaders.

I left Rome with uneasiness about what I had seen. I retained respect for the glory of Catholicism. I admired it as an anthropologist admires a recently discovered but long lost civilization. However, I believed that Rome's amazing superstitions were not those of Paul. I felt sure that if Saint Paul were transported from back in time to contemporary Rome, he would not feel at home with the gold ceilings and marble altars.

I wish that I could write that this trip to Rome kindled a growing love for Catholicism, and that I began my journey toward the Catholic Church after this visit. Rather, my life moved in the opposite direction. My curiosity led me to study theology more precisely. To my horror I found that Catholicism was not merely "superstitious." I naively concluded that it was idolatrous and dangerous. I began to believe that Catholicism was devolution of Christianity since it taught people to worship bread, worship images, and worship the Blessed Virgin Mary. As I studied Paul's epistles I could find no common ground between the religion of Paul and the religion of Rome.

A few years later, I traveled to Greece and was once again confronted with a "foreign Christianity" in the form of Eastern Orthodoxy. Intrigued at first, I soon realized that the Eastern Churches held much in common with Catholicism: saints, sacraments, altars, priests, and incense. I felt like weeping over the city of Athens, and I recalled the parenthetical words of Saint Luke regarding Paul's visit to Athens:

> Now whilst Paul waited for them at Athens, his spirit was stirred within him, seeing the city wholly given to idolatry (Acts 17:16).

I wrote in my journal that night, "Athens is still a 'city full of idols'—only now they call the idols *icons*." As you know, the Eastern Church has a profound devotion to the two dimensional icons that are revered as windows to heaven. As I entered churches and saw worshipers kissing them, I felt once again that I was in the presence of a deformed Christianity.

I went to the site of the Areopagus in Athens, where Saint Paul had first preached the Gospel to the Athenians, and I prayed that the city would once again return to Saint Paul's so-called Protestant message: the justification of sinners by *faith alone*.

Before leaving the city, I noticed a monument erected to a deceased bishop of Athens. The inscription on the monument was written in Greek, which I was able to read. Today, I cannot recall the text of the inscription perfectly. However, it referred to the city's cathedral as a ἱερόν (pronounced *hieron*)—meaning "temple" in Greek. To my horror, the inscription also referred to the city's bishop as a ἀρχιερεύς (pronounced *archiereus*)—meaning "high priest" in Greek. In my mind, the identification of churches as "temples" and clergy as "priests" was tantamount to returning to the Jewish Old Testament—something expressly forbidden by Saint Paul.

So from that time, I considered everything Catholic and priestly as fundamentally contrary to the teaching of Saint Paul. However, the Holy Spirit did not leave me in that state. After studying the Scriptures in Greek and Hebrew and reading the early Church Fathers in their historical context, I began to see that my original conclusions were too hasty. I soon began to see that my prejudices against Catholic Christianity were unfounded. After an extended journey in which I examined the Jewish Origins of Christianity, I came to see that Paul was in fact Catholic. I soon afterward embraced the Catholic Faith, the Faith of Saint Peter and Saint Paul. This book presents this "Catholic Perspective on Paul." It's not a new perspective on Paul. In fact, it's the oldest perspective on Paul—a perspective that is almost two thousand years old.

INTRODUCTION

G.K. CHESTERTON ONCE OBSERVED that the Catholic Church has been "attacked on all sides and for all contradictory reasons. No sooner had one rationalist demonstrated that it was too far to the east than another demonstrated with equal clearness that it was much too far to the west."[1] The same may be said of Saint Paul. The history of heresy is essentially a series of contradictory positions, each claiming the authority of the Apostle Paul.

According to some heretics, Paul was the first corrupter of the life and doctrines of Jesus Christ. To others Paul alone preserved the true message of Christ that had been corrupted by the Twelve. Some consider Paul to have been the champion of grace, while others accuse him of yielding to the so-called Jewish legalism of Peter and James. Paul has since been accused of being too Greek, too Jewish, too gnostic, and too orthodox.

In his own day, he was held by some to be an apostle and by others to be a heretic. Martin Luther claimed Paul's authority, as did the Catholic Council of Trent. He has been called both a misogynist and a liberator of women. Some hail him as a proponent of freedom and others revile him for imposing rules against sexual freedom and social progress. Always and everywhere, Paul is pulled and tugged in opposite directions. Paul has been stretched out so thinly that his features have become faint, almost forgotten.

Prophetically, Saint Peter aptly described the controversial nature of Paul's epistles:

> Also our most dear brother Paul, according to the wisdom given him, hath written to you: As also in all his epistles, speaking in them of these things; in which are certain things hard to be understood, which the unlearned and unstable wrest, as they do also the other Scriptures, to their own destruction (2 Pet 3:15-16).

All the detractors of Paul stand united in their conviction that the historical Paul is certainly not the same Paul revered by the Catholic Church. There is today a deep prejudice against the so-called "Saint Paul" of the Catholic Church. They will grant that Paul was a rabbi, missionary, mystic, polemicist, author, and apostle. However, they will not grant that the man enshrined in the mosaics, statues, and stained glass of a thousand Catholic cathedrals is the Paul of history. The critics are convinced that the Catholic religion as we know it today has little to do with the historic Paul of Tarsus.

The book in your hands seeks to show that this prejudice is just that—a prejudice against a man defined by his own words. Paul is none other than a saint of the Holy Roman and Catholic Church. He spent his life wishing to bring his feet within the walls of Rome and he surrendered his head to the sword outside those very walls. Within his writings, we find the primitive and pristine doctrines of the Catholic Faith. We discover a Paul who is Catholic, a theologian who is sacramental, a churchman who is hierarchical, a mystic who is orthodox.

The Primitive Heresy of Marcion

Scarcely one hundred years had passed after the death of Paul before he was seized upon by one of the most systematic heretics in the history of the Church. Marcion was the son of a bishop near the Black Sea who began teaching publicly some time near A.D. 140. Marcion affirmed that Jesus Christ was the savior of mankind sent by a benevolent God. However, Marcion believed that the God of the Jews was not the God of the Christians. Instead, he believed that the god of Israel was a malicious lower deity whom he identified as the Platonic *demiurge*. Marcion rejected the Old Testament as the horrific history of a capricious god that had created the world and subjected it to unbearable laws. According to Marcion's gospel, a higher and more compassionate God sent his son Jesus Christ to free us from the bondage of the demiurge. Marcion's doctrine of salvation consisted in deliverance from the tyranny of the demiurge's created world, as well as the corrupt apparatus of Judaism that had been instituted by the demiurge.

Marcion held that the twelve disciples of Christ had corrupted the "true gospel" through their Jewish legalism, and that Paul alone had preserved the message of Jesus Christ. Consequently, Marcion believed that Paul, and Paul alone, was the true interpreter of Christ's message. For Marcion, Paul was simply *the* Apostle. Consequently, Marcion and his followers accepted only the writings of Paul and only the Gospel according to Luke, since Luke had been a disciple of Paul. However, even the Marcionite version of Luke's Gospel was modified by Marcion in order to cater to his anti-Jewish presuppositions. Take for example the canonical passage in Luke where Christ rebukes the two disciples on the road to Emmaus:

> O foolish and hard of heart to believe in *all that the prophets have spoken* (Lk 24:25).

Marcion edited this verse in Luke to reflect his anti-Semitic bias:

> O foolish and hard of heart to believe in *all that I have spoken to you* (Marcion's version of Lk 24:25).[2]

One can see from his slight of hand that Marcion rejected the Old Testament prophets as misled servants of the demiurge. Marcion would follow this same prejudice as he read the epistles of Paul. He would emphasize Paul's teaching that the New Covenant surpasses the Old Covenant. Similar to heretics of a later age, Marcion favored the epistle to the Galatians as the primary epistle of Paul. Marcion even placed Galatians as the first book in his biblical canon.

Marcion traveled to Rome and donated to the Church of Rome a gift of two hundred thousand sesterces—the equivalent of several million US dollars in today's economy.[3] Yet, Pope Saint Pius I returned the money to Marcion and formally excommunicated him for his heretical doctrines. On another occasion, Marcion introduced himself to Polycarp, the Catholic bishop of Smyrna. Saint Irenaeus preserves the account of their brief exchange:

> Marcion met Polycarp on one occasion and said, "Do you know me?"
>
> Polycarp responded, "Yes, I know you to be the first-born of Satan!"[4]

Clearly, the leaders of the second-century Church identified Marcion's teaching as something novel and dangerous. Yet, the Marcionites were a force to be reckoned with well into the third century. The Marcionites possessed an organized hierarchy, systematic theology, and biblical canon. Nevertheless, the heresy seems to have fizzled out completely by the fifth century.

Martin Luther's "Protestant Paul"

After the condemnation of Marcion in the second century, the Catholic Church continued to hold that Paul and the other Twelve Apostles proclaimed a unified message—the Gospel of Jesus Christ. This consensus remained unchallenged until the protests of Martin Luther and the subsequent Protestant Reformation of the sixteenth century. Martin Luther was an Augustinian monk and a Catholic priest who bore a troubled conscience. He came to feel oppressed by the unshakable conviction that he could never merit the love of God. As he lectured through Saint Paul's epistles to the Romans and Galatians, he came to believe that Paul presented a gospel that was wholly different than the one taught by the Catholic Church. Whereas, the Catholic Church taught that Christ came to redeem man by infusing grace into the soul of man so that he might *become* holy through faith, hope, charity, and works, Luther taught that a man was justified by faith *alone*.

Luther felt that he was as devout as any Christian could be. He was a bible scholar. He was a priest. He was an Augustinian monk. Luther believed that his new religious epiphany corresponded to Paul's own drastic conversion from Judaism to Christianity. Since the time of Luther, the Protestant tradition has unwittingly read Paul in the same way—through the lens of Martin Luther. The narrative of Luther's conversion is so well canonized in the Protestant tradition that magisterial Protestants often cannot help but think of Paul as a sort of primitive Luther; and the Law of Moses as the corpus of Catholic tradition; and the Jewish apparatus of legalism as the Catholic Church itself. Whether they intend to or not, many read Luther's anti-Catholic rhetoric into Paul's arguments.

The Protestant conjunction of Paul's conversion with Luther's conversion is like one transparency layered on top of another. It is sometimes difficult to tell them apart. This Lutheran fascination with Paul can lead to a latent Marcionite method in theology, that is, to a tendency that elevates Paul at the expense of the other apostles. By this we mean that Protestant sermons and Bible studies focus more on Paul's epistles than they do on the four Gospels depicting the teaching, life, death, and resurrection of Christ.

Contrast this to the Catholic practice. In every celebration of the Holy Sacrifice of the Mass, all present stand to their feet for the reading of the Holy Gospel. Next, all present make the sign of the cross upon their foreheads, lips, and chests—that the Gospel might remain in their minds, mouths, and hearts. The Catholic Church shows greatest honor to the four canonical Gospels (Matthew, Mark, Luke, and John) since these books contain the very words of Christ. Unfortunately, the four Gospels do not hold the esteemed place in Protestantism that they do in the Catholic Church. Instead, Paul is primary in Protestantism. Other biblical authors (especially James!) are cited less frequently. A Protestant friend of mine once remarked, "If all we had were the four Gospels and none of Paul's writings, we would not be able to understand the true Gospel." The Catholic Church naturally disagrees with this sentiment.

Interestingly enough, the Catholic Church opposed Martin Luther not by retreating from Paul, but by rallying to Paul's epistles at the Council of Trent (1545-1563). There has never been a more "Pauline" council in the history of the Catholic Church. The canons and decrees of the Council of Trent repeatedly cite and reference the writings of Paul. In this case, the Council of Trent served Protestantism a healthy dose of its own medicine. However, the Catholic Church did not present the "Lutheran Paul" filtered through Luther's interpretation of Romans and Galatians, but a Paul in harmony with the entire corpus of Paul's writings, along with the rest of the New Testament. When the Council of Trent finally ended, the fathers of the council solemnly invoked "the indignation of Almighty God and of his blessed apostles, Peter and Paul," upon the divisive misinterpreters of Paul.

The Modern Liberal Agenda against Paul

In the nineteenth century, an entirely new challenge was levied against the traditional Catholic perspective on Saint Paul. Following the philosophy of Hegel, the German theologian F.C. Baur (1792-1860) suggested that the primitive Catholic Church was actually the ingenious synthesis of two contrary versions of Christianity.

Recalling the influence of the second-century heretic Marcion and the unshakable resistance of the Roman Church against Marcion, Baur suggested that the first one hundred years of Christianity began as an antithesis between Judaizing Christians who followed Peter and James on the one hand, and anti-Judaizing Christians who followed Paul on the other hand. Baur believed that Christ and the original twelve apostles were Messianic Jews who followed the Law of Moses.

Paul came afterward and took up for himself the title of "Apostle." Paul then proceeded to create a *new* form of Christianity that was thoroughly opposed to the so-called primitive Jewish Christianity of the original apostles. Baur believed that Marcion and his devotees were not actual heretics, but the true followers of the "historical Paul."

Baur suggested that sometime around A.D. 100, Christian leaders created legends that yoked together the alleged twelve "pro-Jewish" Apostles with the alleged "pro-Gentile" Apostle Paul. The centerpiece for this great synthesis, according to Baur, was the work we know as the Acts of the Apostles. Baur believed that Luke did not write this document, but that early Christian leaders stitched together a false history that united two opposing versions of Christianity. The canonical Acts of the Apostles accomplishes this feat, Baur explained, by splicing together the Jewish ministries of Peter and the Apostles with the so-called anti-Jewish ministry of Paul. According to Baur, these same synthesizers also falsely composed the Pastoral Epistles of Paul (1 Timothy, 2 Timothy, Titus) in order to suggest that Paul favored Jewish legalism, hierarchy, and church structure. Baur questioned the authenticity of any epistle attributed to Paul if it spoke of the church, formal church leaders, or any epistle that favored tradition or rules. As a result, Baur rejected not only 1 Timothy, 2 Timothy, and Titus, but also Ephesians, Colossians, and 2 Thessalonians. In addition, Baur unabashedly denied the historical accuracy of the Acts of the Apostles. Baur even dared to suggest that the "false apostles" condemned by Paul in Corinth were actually Peter and the other Apostles!

Liberal biblical theologians today share many of Baur's prejudices to a greater or lesser extent. In academia, Baur's conviction concerning the forged origins of Ephesians, Colossians, 2 Thessalonians, 1 Timothy, 2 Timothy, and Titus is still widely presumed. In many academic circles, one would be openly ridiculed for holding the belief that Paul was the author of the epistle to Titus.

If we seriously examine Baur's hypothesis, we see that it is riddled with Protestant prejudices. Baur assumes, along with Luther, that Paul is opposed to James. He also assumes that Paul is opposed to rules, sacraments, and a hierarchical church. However, Baur and Luther have put the cart before the horse. They have imagined Paul in their own image. They created that for which they had been looking. They have cut and pasted the epistles of Paul until they concocted a Paul that fit their schemes. This is not responsible scholarship and it is not the Catholic way.

The Method of This Book

The method of this book questions the methods of Marcion, Luther, and Baur. Instead, we give credence to the textual tradition. We acknowledge the corpus of Paul's epistles as genuinely Pauline in authorship. Granted, the epistles of Paul bear different styles in places. Yet, we also observe from Paul's own writings that Paul did not in fact "write" all of his epistles. He used secretaries or *amanuenses*, as did nearly all authors in antiquity, as for example Cicero. The epistle to the Romans bears the line: "I Tertius, the writer of this letter, greet you in the Lord" (Rom 16:22). In other words, Paul's epistle to the Romans was *written* by Tertius, but *authored* by Paul. The same is true of the other epistles that often bear the greeting of "Paul and Timothy" (2 Cor, Phil, Col) or "Paul and Sosthenes" (1 Cor).

Paul seems to have been losing his eyesight (Gal 4:15), and it therefore makes sense that he would author his epistles by using his assistants as secretaries. We might assume that Luke the physician performed this duty for Paul in the apostle's final years, since Paul himself admits, "Luke alone is with me" (2 Tim 4:11). In fact, the style and vocabulary of Paul's last three epistles (1 Timothy, 2 Timothy, and Titus) bear some similarities to those books authored by Luke (Gospel of Luke and Acts of the Apostles). Catholic tradition also holds that Luke redacted the final version of the anonymous epistle to the Hebrews on Paul's behalf, a view endorsed by Saint Thomas Aquinas.[5]

For the argument's sake and for rhetorical purposes, this book assumes the posture of Marcion. I have attempted to restrict all theological arguments to the Pauline books of the New Testament. From time to time, I cite the Old Testament or other New Testament passages, but I make it my aim to argue the case for a "Catholic Paul" by sticking to Pauline material.

I consider there to be three strata of Pauline texts in the New Testament. On the first level are those thirteen epistles that explicitly bear the name of Paul and claim to be authored by Paul:

Romans	Colossians
1 Corinthians	1 Thessalonians
2 Corinthians	2 Thessalonians
Galatians	1 Timothy
Ephesians	2 Timothy
Philippians	Titus
Philemon	

On the second level, I place the epistle to the Hebrews. I realize that this work does not explicitly bear the name of Paul, but Catholic tradition holds it to be at least

Pauline, even if the Apostle did not personally give the letter its final form.

On the third level, I place the Gospel of Luke and the Acts of the Apostles since Saint Luke was a close and intimate disciple of Saint Paul. There is not one ancient source doubting Luke's authorship of Gospel of Luke or the Acts of the Apostles. Early sources, such as the Muratorian Fragment, Irenaeus,[6] Tertullian,[7] and Clement of Alexandria[8] affirm that Luke was the author of the Gospel of Luke and the Acts of the Apostles. Although these two works are not strictly Pauline, they do reveal the theology of a man that lived and worked with Paul on a daily, weekly, and yearly basis. Luke no doubt reflects the sentiments and convictions of his master. For this reason, I place Luke's Gospel and Acts on the third and lowest tier of "Pauline documents."

Weighing each of these sources, the balance tips toward Paul being a Catholic, or rather that the Catholic Church is what she is because she is faithful to the Apostle Paul. In Paul, we find a man who is very much like a Catholic priest. He speaks of his ministry as being "priestly" (Rom 15:6). He is proudly and openly celibate (1 Cor 7:7-9). He calls himself "father" (1 Cor 4:15). You will find this volume filled with examples of Paul's Catholic teachings as they relate to the attributes of the Church, the role of faith and works, baptismal regeneration, the sacrament of confirmation, the Eucharistic Real Presence of Christ, purgatory, marriage, moral issues, and even the significance of Rome for the Catholic Church. Through this journey, we find that Saint Paul is in fact a Catholic priest.

Taylor R. Marshall
June 29, 2010

Solemnity of Saint Peter
and Saint Paul

NOTES

[1] G.K. Chesterton, *Orthodoxy* (Wheaton, Illinois: Harold Shaw Publishers, 1994), 89.

[2] For a discussion of Marcion's version of the Gospel of Luke, see David Salter Williams' "Reconsidering Marcion's Gospel," *Journal of Biblical Literature* 108 (1989): 477-96.

[3] This is a reliable interpretation of "currency exchange" since a Roman legionary received a stipend of about one thousand two hundred sesterces per year in the second century.

[4] Saint Irenaeus, *Against Heresies* 3, 3, 4.

[5] See the preface to Saint Thomas Aquinas' *Commentary on the Epistle to the Hebrews*.

[6] Saint Irenaeus of Lyons, *Against Heresies* 3.1.1, 3.14.1.

[7] Tertullian, *Against Marcion* 4.2.2.

[8] Clement of Alexandria, *Paedagogus* 2.1.15; *Stromata* 5.12.82.

1. RABBI SAUL AND THE APOSTLE PAUL

Rabbi Saul

WHAT WE KNOW ABOUT Saint Paul's early life comes from Saint Luke's Acts of the Apostles. He was born in Tarsus in Cilicia (Acts 21:39), which is located in what is today eastern Turkey. His parents were Israelites of the tribe of Benjamin (Phil 3:5), and he was named *Saul* after Israel's first king who also was of the tribe of Benjamin. Saul was born with the prestigious privilege of being a Roman citizen, which entails that his father had also been a Roman citizen (Acts 22:26-28).

We know little of Saul's parents. Saint Jerome records a tradition that his parents were natives of Gischala in Galilee and moved to Tarsus before his birth.[9] If this tradition were true, we might conclude that Saul's kin were Galileans just as the other Apostles had been Galileans. We know that Saul's family was pious and devout (2 Tim 1:3) and that he had been a follower of the traditions of the Pharisees (Phil 3:5-6).

As for his education, Saul's parents had sent him as a boy to study Torah in Jerusalem. We also read that Saul had a sister who resided in Jerusalem (Acts 23:16). As a young man, Saul sat at the feet of the renowned Rabbi Gamaliel (Acts 22:3). Gamaliel was the grandson of one of the greatest Jewish scholars in Jewish history—Hillel who died around A.D. 10. Hillel is the founder of the intellectual dynasty culminating in the Jewish *Mishnah*—the first record of oral law for Rabbinical Judaism.

The sect of the Pharisees was itself divided into two schools—the followers of Hillel and the followers of Shammai. Shammai interpreted the Jewish law more strictly than Hillel did. The classic example used to show the differences between the school of Hillel and the school of Shammai is that Hillel permitted divorce liberally (for example, a man could divorce his wife if she burned dinner), whereas Shammai did not permit divorce. Paul conforms to the latter belief (Rom 7:2-3, see also CHAPTER NINE). Hillel served as the president of the Sanhedrin until his death in A.D. 10 when Shammai succeeded him to the office of president of the Sanhedrin. When Shammai died in A.D. 30, Hillel's grandson Gamaliel was elected president.

Paul claims to have studied under Gamaliel (Acts 22:3). This does not, however, entail that Saul was a follower of Hillel. N.T. Wright is correct in identifying Saul with the Shammaite Pharisees.[10] Wright observes that Gamaliel, who represented the Hillelites, was tolerant of Christianity, whereas Saul sought to murder the early Christians. Perhaps Saul did study under Gamaliel and later became an adherent of Shammai. Another suggestion is that Gamaliel was unique in his toleration of Christianity.

Catholic tradition subsequently identified Gamaliel as an undercover Christian, even as a Catholic saint. This belief arose from Gamaliel's toleration of the incipient Christian movement. Saint Luke records how Gamaliel appealed to the Jewish Sanhedrin on behalf of the Apostles:

> But a Pharisee in the council named Gamaliel, a teacher of the law, held in honor by all the

people, stood up and ordered the men to be put outside for a while. And he said to them: "Men of Israel, take care what you do with these men. So in the present case I tell you, keep away from these men and let them alone. For if this plan or this undertaking is of men, it will fail. However, if it is of God, you will not be able to overthrow them. You might even be found opposing God!" (Acts 5:34-35, 38-39)

Thus, Gamaliel played a key role in convincing the Sanhedrin to free the Apostles (Acts 5:40).

The *Clementine Recognitions* describes Gamaliel's secret allegiance with the early Christians and with Saint James of Jerusalem in particular. According to this document, Gamaliel received a special dispensation from the Apostles allowing him to profess faith in Christ privately so that he might then inform the Apostles about the Sanhedrin's plans of persecution:

> Then, when profound silence was obtained, Gamaliel, who, as we have said, was of our faith, but who by a dispensation remained among them, that if at any time they should attempt anything unjust or wicked against us, he might either check them by skillfully adopted counsel, or might warn us, that we might either be on our guard or might turn it aside.[11]

Hence, the Roman Martyrology of the Catholic Church describes Gamaliel as a saint of the Catholic Church in its account for commemorations on the date August 3:

> At Jerusalem, the body of Blessed Stephen the Protomartyr, and the bodies of Saint Gamaliel, Saint Nicodemus, and Saint Abibo were found

through a divine revelation made to the priest Lucian, in the time of Emperor Honorius.[12]

Catholic art also depicts Gamaliel and Nicodemus as those who orchestrated the burial of Saint Stephen after his martyrdom.[13] The relics of Gamaliel are still venerated at the Cathedral of Pisa (known for its famous leaning tower).

Saint John Chrysostom relates that Gamaliel converted to Christianity before Saint Paul was baptized.[14] Moreover, the presbyter Lucian testifies that Saint Gamaliel appeared to him several times beginning on the third day of December in A.D. 415. He appeared to Lucian as a bearded man, wearing a white robe, and holding a golden staff. "I am Gamaliel" the apparition explained, "who instructed the Apostle Paul in the Law." In the vision, Gamaliel described how he laid the body of Saint Stephen in his own tomb. Next, Gamaliel revealed to Lucian the site of this same tomb outside Jerusalem where the bodies of Nicodemus, Gamaliel, and Gamaliel's son also rested. Following the directions of Gamaliel, the presbyter Lucian discovered the tomb and the relics within. When the relics were found, the people in the region of Jerusalem flocked to the site and many were cured of various maladies.

Lest we dismiss this account as exaggerated hagiography, it's worth noting that Saint Augustine, a contemporary witness to these events, confirms the mysterious discovery of Saint Stephen's relics.[15] Bishop Ovodius, a close friend of Saint Augustine, also published a work titled *The Miracles of Saint Stephen,* which depends on the same account described above. Furthermore, Saint Augustine records how his diocese of Hippo received relics of Saint Stephen from the tomb miraculously discovered by Lucian, and he also records the miracles wrought by these relics.[16] The testimony seems to confirm that Gamaliel appeared in the fifth century as a Catholic saint from heaven.

Whether or not Gamaliel was a Christian before or after Paul converted, Gamaliel nevertheless exerted influence on the adolescent Saul—perhaps more than Saul originally comprehended. Saul's relationship with the respected Rabbi Gamaliel gained him entry into the upper echelons of the religious authorities in Jerusalem. He stood by and "held the coats" of the men who killed Stephen the Deacon in Jerusalem for the charge of being a Christian. In the biblical account of the murder of Saint Stephen, Saul is called a *neanias*, a Greek term indicating that he was a "young man" in his twenties at the time.

As a Pharisee, Saul possessed a vehement hatred of the early Christians who at this time were called "the followers of the Way" (Act 19:9). The Pharisees held fast to the traditions of the elders and rejected the Christian claim that Jesus of Nazareth was the Messiah and the Son of God who had been raised from the dead. The Pharisees, whose name means *pure ones*, believed that God would liberate the Jewish people and reunite the twelve tribes of Israel by sending the Messiah only when the people of Israel had purified themselves and dutifully observed the works of the Law of Moses.

The newly formed sect of the Christians rejected the central tenets of the Pharisees. The Christians taught that Jesus is the Messiah, and that He had already established the Kingdom of God by ascending to the right hand of God the Father. Moreover, Christians believed that the reunification of the twelve tribes of Israel would also incorporate all the gentile nations. One can understand how Saul's blood boiled when he with the other Pharisees heard Stephen accuse them of being spiritually uncircumcised and persecutors of the prophets:

> You stiff-necked people, uncircumcised in heart and ears, you always resist the Holy Spirit. As your fathers did, so do you. Which of the prophets did not your fathers persecute? And they killed those who announced beforehand the coming of the Righteous One, whom you have now betrayed and murdered, you who received the law as delivered by angels and did not keep it (Acts 7:51-53).

Given the convictions of the Pharisees, we can also understand why Saul gladly stood by as his comrades executed this Christian "blasphemer." Yet Stephen's death did not satiate Paul's anger against the Christians. Saul went to the High Priest, "breathing threats and murder against the disciples of the Lord," and obtained authority to hunt down and capture Christians outside Jerusalem (Acts 9:1). Having received authorization, Rabbi Saul set out to arrest Christians in Damascus. Little did Saul know that he would arrive in Damascus as the world's most recent convert to the sect he previously had sought to destroy.

Apostle Paul

Many people believe that Paul was knocked off his horse on the road to Damascus. Caravaggio's famous painting titled "Conversion on the Way to Damascus" has seared into our imaginations the image that Paul fell in amazement from his horse when Christ appeared to him in the midst of a blinding light. However, if you go back and read the biblical account of the miracle, nowhere does it describe Saul falling off his horse. In fact, we can be certain that Rabbi Saul was *not* on his horse at midday when Christ appeared to him (Acts 26:13). We know this because Pharisees prayed regularly throughout the day in obedience to Psalm 55:16-17, "But I call upon God, and the LORD will save me. Evening and morning and at noon." Jewish men recited these prayers standing on their feet and facing toward Jerusalem. Saul no doubt observed noonday prayer on that day as he traveled along the road to Damascus. He was likely standing erect and facing south to Jerusalem when Jesus Christ spoke to him and blinded him with light. Paul described the experience like this:

> I heard a voice saying to me in the Hebrew language, 'Saul, Saul, why do you persecute me? It hurts you to kick against the goads.'
>
> And I said, 'Who are you, Lord?'
>
> And the Lord said, 'I am Jesus whom you are persecuting. But rise and stand upon your feet; for I have appeared to you for this purpose, to appoint you to serve and bear witness to the things in which you have seen me and to those in which I will appear to you, delivering you from the people and from the Gentiles to whom I send you to open their eyes, that they may turn from darkness to light and from the power of Satan to God, that they may receive forgiveness of sins and a place among those who are sanctified by faith in me' (Acts 26:14-18).

Blinded by this brilliant apparition of Christ, Saul went to Damascus where the very Christians whom he had sought to imprison received him. A Christian leader in Damascus by the name of Ananias laid his hands on Saul, and at once the one-time persecutor of the

Christians received back his sight. Saul then received the sacrament of baptism. Incidentally, Saul was baptized in a home and not in a river (Acts 9:17-18). As might be expected, the Christians of Damascus were not eager to receive Saul into their fellowship. "Is not this the man who made havoc in Jerusalem of those who called on this name? And he has come here for this purpose, to bring them bound before the chief priests" (Act 9:21). However, Saul's conversion proved genuine as he immediately began to proclaim that Jesus was the promised Messiah of Israel.

I cannot help but wonder whether Saul contemplated Stephen's dying words of forgiveness as he traveled along the road to Damascus. Perhaps Saul began to contemplate Stephen's claims in light of his comprehensive knowledge of the Hebrew Scriptures. Saul had dedicated his life to studying the Messianic promises of God to the people of Israel, and on that day at noon, the Messiah Himself appeared to him. Although his eyes became blind, his heart became filled with light. Was Saul horrified by how wrong he had been? Was he delighted to know that God's promises had been fulfilled in Jesus of Nazareth? We only know that he reacted by transforming his zeal into a fiery love for Christ.

It has been said that Paul's entire theology is an expansion upon the particular words of Christ pronounced to him on the road to Damascus: "Saul, Saul, why do you persecute *me*?" (Acts 26:14). With these words, Christ revealed that to persecute any of His disciples is to persecute Him. When Saul approved of the murder of Stephen, he had approved of the murder of Christ. When Saul imprisoned Christians, he had imprisoned Christ. From this intimate union between Christ and his disciples, Saint Paul extrapolated his entire theological system. Accordingly, Paul's doctrine of the believer's union with the person of Christ is the bedrock of Catholic theology because it presents salvation in terms of *participation*. Christ's statement to Saul reveals that the Christian believer participates in the life of Christ. This is the center of Paul's message. "So we, though many, are one body in Christ, and individually members one of another" (Rom 12:5). The epistles of Paul constantly and consistently resound with the phrase "in Christ" and "in Him." This phrase is more common than any other topic in the letters of Paul *combined*. This means that Paul discusses the believer's participation in Christ more than justification, faith, works, law, or predestination. Union with Christ is the ubiquitous theme of Paul's theology.

When we understand Christianity as a participation in Christ, we begin to read Paul's epistles in a new light, or rather under the ancient light of the Church Fathers who lived before us. We find that the "old perspective on Paul" articulated by the Catholic Church had it correct all along. Saint Paul presents the church, baptism, the Eucharist, marriage, faith, works, justification, sanctification, and regeneration as participations in the person and work of Christ. As we shall see, this interpretation confirms that Paul's teachings are in fact the teachings of the Catholic Church.

Paul's Doctrine of Participation in Christ

Paul's paradigm of "union with Christ" can be contrasted with what I call "zero-sum theology." Let me boldly suggest that all theological misunderstandings regarding the Catholic Faith can be attributed to the adoption of zero-sum theology, that is, a framework that views salvation, grace, life, and love as a pie with only so many pieces. Christ either gets all pieces or loses the remaining pieces to Mary, saints, sacraments, priests, popes, etc. Naturally, Christ as God should receive all the pieces—not merely some of the pieces. He is the whole of salvation, right?

Of course, Christ is the whole. He is "all in all" as Saint Paul beautifully teaches (Eph 1:23). However, Catholics do not subscribe to a zero-sum approach to Christ. Instead, Catholicism embraces Saint Paul's paradigm of participation. Christ is "all in all," but this means that all other aspects of redemption participate in and through Christ—not apart from Christ. Catholics thus believe that the sacraments, Mary, saints, and priests participate in and through Christ, and thereby lead the Christian to embrace Christ more deeply.

This difference between Catholicism and Protestantism accounts for almost every doctrinal difference between Catholic theology and Protestant theology. Catholicism is framed by a doctrine of participation—Protestantism is generally framed by the zero-sum paradigm. To help us better appreciate how the doctrine of participation in Christ plays out in the realm of human salvation, let us look at the historical controversies surrounding the doctrine of grace.

How are We Saved by Grace?

Are people saved by grace alone to the exclusion of all human effort and activity? This question has been argued back and forth for centuries. I have outlined below four possible answers to this question: Does God accomplish salvation or does man *add* something?

> 100% God & 0% man (Calvinism, Jansenism)
> 99% God & 1% man (Arminianism)
> 50% God & 50% man (Semi-Pelagianism)

0% God & 100% man (Pelagianism)

The Catholic Church rejects all four of the above solutions. Instead, the Catholic Church posits the following solution:

100% God & 100% man (Augustine, Aquinas)

As Saint Augustine confirms:

> Now, concerning His working that we may will, it is said: "It is God who works in you, even to will" (Phil 2:13). While of His co-working with us, when we will and act by willing, the Apostle says, "We know that in all things there is co-working for good to them that love God" (Rom 8:28).[17]

Augustine focuses on Paul's words in Philippians 2:3 stressing that God *works within us*. God's operation and our cooperation are intimately related. Following Saint Augustine, Saint Thomas Aquinas also held that grace is fittingly divided into operating and cooperating grace.[18]

The Catholic Church articulates human salvation in terms of operation and cooperation because it perceives human salvation *in union with Christ*. By becoming united to Christ, the Holy Spirit takes us up into Christ's love for the Father. Christ has a divine will and a human will working together in perfect synergy.[19] Just as Christ's human will cooperated with the divine will, so we also unite our human wills to the will of God: "thy kingdom come, thy will be done" (Mt 6:10). God does not accomplish the work of salvation without us: Christ is crucified, but we are also crucified "in Him." As Saint Augustine once remarked: "God created us without us, but he did not will to save us without us."[20] God is entirely responsible for our salvation, but we too play a part by participating in His work. For Catholics, salvation is not "God *and* me," but rather, "God *in* me." There is no contradiction in that. Paul teaches the same:

> And I live, now not I: but Christ lives in me. And that I live now in the flesh: I live in the faith of the Son of God, who loved me and delivered himself for me (Gal 2:20).

Paul's sufferings are not viewed apart from Christ's suffering. It is not that Christ performs 95% and Paul provides 5%. Rather, Paul explains "Christ lives in me." There is now a complete union of Christ and Paul so that the work of Christ echoes through the actions of Paul. Christ is fully active and Paul is fully active through a cooperative synergy. Nowadays the word *synergy* carries with it an economic connotation, so do not let that confuse you. The word *synergy* comes from the Greek word *synergia*—a word used by Saint Paul to mean literally "working together."[21] For example, the Apostle writes:

> *Working together* {*synergountes*} with Him, then, we entreat you not to accept the grace of God in vain (2 Cor 6:1).

This "synergy" of Christ in believers is based firmly on the grace of God. Christ's life echoes in the lives of those closest to Christ. This is why Christ asked Saul, "Why do you persecute *me*?" when Paul and others murdered Saint Stephen. The martyrdom of Stephen is a reverberation of the passion and death of Christ. Stephen's sufferings do not compete with Christ's sufferings. Rather, Stephen's sufferings (and the sufferings of all the saints) participate in the sufferings of Christ and extend the passion of Christ throughout time.

If we understand salvation in terms of synergy, then we can also appreciate the role of sacraments and human agency in salvation. An Evangelical might object and say, "Baptism does not save you. Jesus saves you." Again, this is the error of zero-sum theology. Why can't baptism participate instrumentally in the redemptive work of Christ and save me? Why must it be "either/or"? We will discuss this difficulty in more detail in the chapter on baptism.

A Protestant might also say, "Christ saves you, not the saints." Yet Paul writes: "I have become all things to all men, that *I might save* some" (1 Cor 9:22). Paul is a saint and he clearly believed that he "saved" people. However, Paul only "saved" people through his participation in the apostolic priesthood of Christ. It is not Jesus vs. Paul—it is Jesus *through* Paul. Here again, Paul shows us that the biblical paradigm is participation, not zero-sum. With this in mind, let us move on to Paul's doctrine of the Catholic Church. Paul's vision of the Church amplifies our understanding of being "in Christ," since Paul defines the Church as the mystical "Body of Christ."

NOTES

[9] Saint Jerome, *De viris illustribus* 5.

[10] N.T. Wright, *What Saint Paul Really Said: Was Paul of Tarsus the Real Founder of Christianity?* (Grand Rapids, Michigan: Eerdmans Publishing Company, 1997), 26.

[11] *Clementine Recognitions* 1, 66.

NOTES CONTINUED

¹² *Roman Martyrology*, August 3. Translation from Latin mine.

¹³ The most notable example is Carlo Saraceni's school version of "Saint Stephen Mourned by Saints Gamaliel and Saint Nicodemus," which is displayed at the Museum of Fine Arts in Boston.

¹⁴ Saint John Chrysostom, *Homily XIV in Act.*

¹⁵ Saint Augustine, *Commentary on St. John,* Tractate 120. Migne also reports that this revelation, whereby the bodies of Saint Stephen and Nicodemus were discovered through the appearance of Saint Gamaliel the Jew, is referred to the close of the year 415, by those who trust in the authority of the Presbyter Lucian, in a small book written on the subject. See also how Photius read in a work of Eustratius recounting how St Peter and St John baptized and initiated Gamaliel.

¹⁶ Saint Augustine, *City of God* 22, 8.

¹⁷ Saint Augustine, *De Gratia et Lib. Arbit.*, 17.

¹⁸ Saint Thomas Aquinas, *Summa theologiae* I-II, q. 111, a. 2. Thomas clarifies that, "Operating and cooperating grace are the same grace; but are distinguished by their different effects."

¹⁹ *Seventh Ecumenical Council* (Nicea II): "We profess, and so we believe that in our one Lord Jesus Christ, our true God, there are two natures unconfusedly, unchangeably, undividedly, and two natural wills and two natural operations; and all who have taught, and who now say, that there is but one will and one operation in the two natures of our one Lord Jesus Christ our true God, we anathematize."

NOTES CONTINUED

[20] Saint Augustine, Sermon 169, 11, 13: *Patrologia Latina* 38, 923.

[21] For Paul's use of *synergeo* see Rom 8:28; 1 Cor 16:16; 2 Cor 6:1.

2. PAUL ON THE CATHOLIC CHURCH

…the Church of the living God,
the pillar and ground of the truth…
1 TIMOTHY 3:15

To UNDERSTAND SAINT PAUL, we must turn immediately to his doctrine of the Church. On the road to Damascus, when Saint Paul realized that he had persecuted Christ by persecuting Christ's Church, he came to understand that the Church is the "Body of Christ" (1 Cor 12:27). As Christians we regularly refer to the Church as the Body of Christ, but consider for a moment how odd it is to refer to a group of people as the "body" of a certain historical person. We sometimes speak of the *body politic*, but we do not often think of societies as a body belonging to a historical personage. America is a body of people, but it is not *the body of George Washington*. However, Saint Paul discovered that the Church is the body of the historical Jesus of Nazareth. Christ mystically incorporates into His own body all those who belong to Him. As a result, the Church bears the attributes of Christ.

In A.D. 325, the Council of Nicea proclaimed the Church to be the "One, Holy, Catholic, and Apostolic Church." Catholic Christians sometimes refer to these attributes as the four marks of the Church. The four marks of the Church are derived almost wholly from the writings of Saint Paul. Christ is one. Therefore, the

Church is one. Christ is holy. Therefore, the Church is holy. Christ is catholic or universal. Therefore, the Church is catholic. Christ founded the Church on His apostles. Therefore, the Church must submit to apostolic teaching and be organically connected to the apostles. These four attributes most fully describe the Church that Christ instituted with the intention that "the gates of hell would not prevail against it" (Mt 16:18).

The Church is One

Saint Paul is resolute in his conviction that the Church of Christ must be one. Most of his epistles specifically speak against disunity within the Church. Paul's First Epistle to the Corinthians seems to have been written for the very purpose of encouraging church unity against the tendency of "church splits."

> I appeal to you, brethren, by the name of our Lord Jesus Christ, that all of you agree and that there be no dissensions among you, but that you be united in the same mind and the same judgment. For it has been reported to me by Chloe's people that there is quarreling among you, my brethren. What I mean is that each one of you says, "I belong to Paul," or "I belong to Apollos," or "I belong to Peter," or "I belong to Christ." Is Christ divided? Was Paul crucified for you? Or were you baptized in the name of Paul?" (1 Cor 1:10-13).

The Apostle's purpose in writing to the Corinthian Christians was, "that there be no divisions" in the Church. Paul could not conceive of Christians naming themselves after human church leaders. Paul exhorted the Corinthians not to tolerate those who claimed to be "Pauline" Christians. Nor should there be any

"Apollonian" Christians or "Petrine" Christians. Given Paul's insistence against name-bearing sects, we might safely conclude that he would fiercely condemn the practice of certain Christians who identify themselves as "Lutherans" or "Calvinists." As a matter of fact, the term "denomination" comes from the Latin *de nomine* meaning "of a name." This *denominational* arrangement is foreign to the teachings of Paul. For this reason, the Catholic Church never accepted a denominational understanding of the Church. The Catholic Church is not a denomination because it does not claim to follow a certain human founder (Luther, Calvin, Wesley, for example) but is the unbroken community of clergy and laity going back to Christ and the Apostles. Not one Protestant congregation on earth can trace its origin to the Apostles.

Notice also how Paul associates "name-calling" with salvation. "Was Paul crucified for you? Or were you baptized in the name of Paul?" (1 Cor 1:13) Recall how Paul understands the Church as a participation in the person and life of Christ. To call oneself "Pauline" or "Lutheran" is to claim participation in the one whose name you bear. While denominational Christians do not think of themselves as participating in a person other than Christ, from Paul's perspective, subscribing to a denomination (for example, Lutheranism) is tantamount to identifying the founder of that denomination (Luther) as the Redeemer, Savior, and Founder of one's faith. In fact, Saint Paul specifically instructed Christians in every case to "avoid those who cause schism" (Rom 16:17). Even if the Church requires renewal, Paul holds that division is not the means to achieve it.

Saint Paul further identifies the unity of the Church with the Holy Spirit. In Ephesians, Paul identifies the unity of the Church with the unity of the Holy Spirit, the unity of Christ, the unity of the faith, the unity of baptism and finally the unity of God the Father. It is difficult to imagine a more compelling argument for the unity of the Church than the one set down by Paul:

> I therefore, a prisoner for the Lord, beg you to lead a life worthy of the calling to which you have been called, with all lowliness and meekness, with patience, forbearing one another in love, eager to maintain the unity of the Spirit in the bond of peace. There is one body and one Spirit, just as you were called to the one hope that belongs to your call, one Lord, one faith, one baptism, one God and Father of us all, who is above all and through all and in all (Eph 4:1-6).

Paul asks Christians to be "eager to maintain the unity of the Spirit." Only the Catholic Church has maintained the unity that Christ established before He ascended into heaven. No other "denomination" is able to claim Paul in this regard. Non-Catholics may claim to be "united in Spirit," but they contradict one another in matters of faith and morals. For example, some denominations baptize infants while others believe it to be incorrect and sinful. Some denominations believe in "once-saved-always-saved," while others teach that one can lose the grace of salvation. Hence, these denominations may claim to be "united in Spirit," but they do not subscribe to the formula of "one faith," as listed by Paul above.

The Church is Holy

The Catholic Church does not maintain that she is "holy" by her own merits. Rather it is Christ who makes the Church holy as Paul describes in his epistle to the Ephesians:

> Husbands, love your wives, as Christ loved the
> Church and gave Himself up for her, that He
> might sanctify her, having cleansed her by the
> washing of water with the word, that he might
> present the Church to Himself in splendor,
> without spot or wrinkle or any such thing, that
> she might be holy and without blemish (Eph 5:25-
> 27).

Because Christ poured out His Holy Spirit upon the
Catholic Church on the day of Pentecost, the Church
itself is the holy People of God, and Saint Paul says that
the Church's members are called to be "saints" (1 Cor
6:1; 16:1). Moreover, Paul identifies the Church as holy by
calling it "the Temple of the Living God" (2 Cor 6:16).

Yet, the Apostle understood that the Church of
Christ consists of sinners. Jesus Christ had established
twelve Apostles, and yet one of them betrayed him. That
means that during the earthly ministry of Christ, there
was an 8.33% rate of clerical failure among the Apostles
(i.e., one out of twelve). In fact, all of the Apostles except
for Saint John abandoned Christ at the crucifixion. If we
reckon that eleven out of twelve fled from the crucifixion,
then that yields a clerical failure rate of 91.67%! Even
Saint Peter, the first Pope, denied Christ three times.
These facts reveal that the Church has consisted of
sinners from the beginning.

For these reasons, the Catholic Church does not
pretend that every pope, bishop, priest, deacon, monk,
nun, and layman is good, holy, and virtuous. A cursory
reading of Church history will confirm that Peter's
threefold denial of Christ and Judas' apostasy were only
the first of many scandals. Clearly, the Church is not holy
because of her members. Rather, the Church is holy
because the Holy Spirit dwells within her. As we will see
in a later chapter, the Church is also holy because she is

united to the saints in heaven who are free from sin and who "surround us as a cloud of witnesses" (Heb 12:1).

The Church is Catholic

There is often confusion over what is meant by the term *catholic*. It comes from the Greek words *kata holos* meaning "according to the whole," denoting that believers hold the whole of doctrine and also to the universality of the Church in all places. The Catholic Church calls herself "catholic" for two reasons. First, the Church of Jesus Christ is catholic because Christ is present within her. Saint Ignatius of Antioch († A.D. 107), a martyr and early disciple of the Apostles, could therefore state, "Where there is Christ Jesus, there is the Catholic Church."[22] The second reason why the Catholic Church identifies herself as *catholic* is that she has been sent out by Christ on a mission to the whole of the human race.

Saint Paul himself never calls the Church "catholic." However, his epistles often describe the universality of the Church: "There is neither Jew nor Greek, there is neither slave nor free, there is neither male nor female; for you are all one in Christ Jesus" (Gal 3:28). Paul also believes that the Church is the instrument by which the message of Christ will become universally known:

> To me, though I am the very least of all the saints, this grace was given, to preach to the Gentiles the unsearchable riches of Christ, and to make all men see what is the plan of the mystery hidden for ages in God who created all things; *that through the Church* the manifold wisdom of God might now be made known to the principalities and powers in the heavenly places (Eph 3:8-10, *emphasis* mine).

Paul did not say that all men would know the plan of salvation *through the Bible*. Rather, Paul said that the manifold wisdom of God would be made known to all nations *through the Church*.

The Church is Apostolic

Before I became Catholic, I remember being unnerved by Saint Paul's words in his First Epistle to Timothy:

> If I am delayed, you may know how one ought to behave in the household of God, which is the Church of the living God, the pillar and bulwark of the truth (1 Tim 3:15).

I must have read those words dozens times on previous occasions, but never did it occur to me that "the Church of the living God" is also "the pillar and bulwark of the truth." Everything changed when I came to see the meaning of Paul's words in this verse. I thought to myself: *If the church is the pillar and bulwark of truth, then it must be something more than I have experienced as a Protestant and as a Anglican.* Paul places all apostolic authority in "the Church of the living God." It is the Church of Jesus Christ on earth that is the guardian of the truth. The Holy Spirit gave the Sacred Scriptures to us, but the Holy Spirit also gave us the Church as the "pillar" that raises it up and as the "bulwark" that protects the truth of divine revelation. Saint Paul does not say that the Bible *alone* is the pillar and bulwark of the truth. I say this without any intention to belittle the authority of the inspired Sacred Scriptures. What I wish to say is that the Scripture's original and proper context is within the interpretation of the Church. The Catholic Church officially teaches that Sacred Scriptures are inspired by God and without error. As Pope Leo XIII declared:

For all the books which the Church receives as sacred and canonical, are written wholly and entirely, with all their parts, at the dictation of the Holy Ghost; and so far is it from being possible that any error can co-exist with inspiration, that inspiration not only is essentially incompatible with error, but excludes and rejects it as absolutely and necessarily as it is impossible that God Himself, the supreme Truth, can utter that which is not true. This is the ancient and unchanging faith of the Church, solemnly defined in the Councils of Florence and of Trent, and finally confirmed and more expressly formulated by the Council of the Vatican.[23]

This conforms perfectly to Saint Paul's teaching on the matter: "All scripture is inspired by God and profitable for teaching, for reproof, for correction, and for training in righteousness, that the man of God may be complete, equipped for every good work" (2 Tim 3:16-17). However, Scripture is "not the matter of one's personal interpretation" (2 Pet 1:20). Therefore, the magisterium of the Catholic Church possesses the sole authority of interpretation. Again, the Catholic Church is not the guardian of the truth on account of the intelligence or holiness of her members. Rather, the Church is the pillar and bulwark of truth because of Christ's solemn promise to Saint Peter:

You are Peter, and on this rock I will build my church, and the gates of hell shall not prevail against it. I will give you the keys of the kingdom of heaven, and whatever you bind on earth shall be bound in heaven, and whatever you loose on earth shall be loosed in heaven (Mt 16:18-19).

The epistle to the Hebrews further assigns apostolic authority to church leaders: "Obey your leaders and submit to them, because they are keeping watch over your souls, as men who will have to give account. Let them do this joyfully, and not sadly, for that would be of no advantage to you" (Heb 13:17). This complements Paul's teaching that the Church of Jesus Christ has the power to excommunicate (1 Cor 5:5; 1 Tim 1:20), a power that the Catholic Church still reluctantly yields. In fact, the tradition of excommunication derives from the Greek formula of Paul "Let him be *anathema.*"

> But even if we, or an angel from heaven, should preach to you a gospel contrary to what we have preached to you, he is to be anathema! (Gal 1:8)

> If anyone does not love the Lord, he is to be anathema (1 Cor 16:22).

We find in the writings of Saint Paul several exhortations to obey the apostolic traditions of the Church. Luke, the disciple and constant companion of Paul, records that the primitive Church was "devoted to the Apostles' teaching and fellowship" (Acts 2:32). The writings of Paul and the witness of Luke reveal that the Church is necessarily apostolic. The Protestant doctrine of "Scripture alone" directly contradicts what Saint Paul taught on Scripture and Apostolic Tradition:

> So then, brethren, stand firm and hold to the traditions, which you were taught by us, either by word of mouth or by letter (2 Thess 2:15).

Here we find that Christians are to "stand firm and hold" to the Sacred Traditions. We find that these traditions come to us either by "word of mouth or by letter." This is the preeminent text supporting the Catholic Church's doctrine that the Word of God comes to us both in oral Tradition and in written Scripture. The Apostle confirms that oral tradition is in fact the "Word of God":

> And we also thank God constantly for this, that when you received the word of God *which you heard from us*, you accepted it not as the word of men but as what it really is, the word of God, which is at work in you believers (1 Thess 2:13).

Saint Paul also commends the Corinthians to "maintain the traditions" of the Apostles:

> I commend you because you remember me in everything and maintain the traditions even as I have delivered them to you (1 Cor 11:2).

And again, Paul exhorts his disciple Timothy to pass on the apostolic tradition to his apostolic successors:

> And what you have heard from me before many witnesses entrust to faithful men who will be able to teach others also (2 Tim 2:2).

Notice how Paul assumes that future leaders in the Church will be equipped by this passing on of Sacred Tradition. The Church is therefore apostolic because she finds herself linked to the apostolic succession of bishops, but also because she has received the apostolic tradition, preserved by the Church, which Paul describes as "the pillar and bulwark of the truth."

We close this chapter with Saint Paul's definitive description of the Church as "one, holy, catholic, and apostolic" from his epistle to the Ephesians:

CHRIST'S CHURCH IS CATHOLIC OR UNIVERSAL
So then, you are *no longer strangers and sojourners*,
but you are *fellow citizens* with the saints and members of
the *household of God* (Eph 2:19)

CHRIST'S CHURCH IS APOSTOLIC
…built upon *the foundation of the apostles and prophets*,
Christ Jesus himself being the cornerstone (Eph 2:20)

CHRIST'S CHURCH IS ONE
…in whom the whole structure *is joined together*
(Eph 2:21a)

CHRIST'S CHURCH IS HOLY
…and grows into a *holy temple* in the Lord,
in whom you also are built into it for
a dwelling place of God in the Spirit (Eph 2:21b-22).

Paul's description of the people of God confirms that they derive from every nation, that their faith is apostolic, that they are united together in one body, and that the Church is a holy temple of God. Consequently, when a Catholic recites the Nicene Creed on any given Sunday, he can be assured that he is confessing the same four marks of the Church that Paul articulated nearly two thousand years ago when he wrote to the Christians in Ephesus.

Those who do not belong to the Catholic Church cannot endorse all four marks of the Church, because the ecclesial communities deriving from the Reformation are man-made denominations that possess neither unity nor apostolic succession. These four attributes belong only to the one Catholic Church because the existence of a second Church would deny the unity of the one Body of Christ. In the next chapter, we will examine how an individual believer shares in this life in a particular way as both a member of Christ and a member of His Body the Church. We turn, then, to the controversial topic of Saint Paul's doctrine of justification.

NOTES

[22] Saint Ignatius of Antioch, *Epistle to the Smyrneans* 8:2.

[23] Pope Leo XIII, *Providentissimus Deus*, 20.

3. PAUL ON JUSTIFICATION, FAITH & WORKS

…faith working through love…
GALATIANS 5:6

Paul and Martin Luther

MARTIN LUTHER LAUNCHED the Reformation with his material principle of "justification by faith *alone.*" Oddly enough, Luther's doctrine of justification by faith alone did not explicitly meet his formal principle that "Scripture alone" is the sole source for Christian doctrine. Luther's difficulty lies in the fact that the words "justification by faith alone" do not appear in the pages of Sacred Scripture. It would seem then that Luther's doctrine of "faith alone" contradicts the criteria of "Scripture alone."

Saint Paul uses the word "alone" more than any other New Testament author, yet he never uses "alone" in conjunction with "faith." Instead, the only place in Sacred Scripture where the word "faith" and the word "alone" exist together is within the epistle of Saint James: "You see that a man is justified by works and *not* by faith alone" (Jas 2:24). Here we find the phrase "faith alone," but it is categorically rejected as the means of our justification. Saint James asserts that Christians are *not* justified by faith alone. For this reason, Martin Luther called the epistle of James "an epistle of straw," and remarked, "I almost feel like throwing Jimmy into the stove."[24] Luther also wrote, "We should throw the epistle of James out of this school, for it doesn't amount to much. It contains not a syllable about Christ."[25] Contrary to Luther's bias toward the epistle of James, Sacred Scripture records that Saint Paul and Saint James were in complete accord with one another at the Council of Jerusalem (cf. Acts 15). Luther jockeyed two inspired New Testament authors against one another in order to create the catalyst for the Protestant Reformation. By doing so, Luther introduced an artificial tension between Saint Paul and the other Apostles of the New Testament.

Martin Luther was aware that Saint Paul never once wrote that we are justified by faith *alone*. For this reason, Luther tampered with the text of Holy Writ. When he translated Saint Paul's epistle to the Romans, he added the German word for "alone" into Romans 3:28. The authentic rendering of Saint Paul's explanation of justification in Romans 3:28 reads this way:

> For we hold that a man is justified by faith apart from works of law.

Whereas Luther translated the verse in this way:

> So halten wir nun dafür, daß der Mensch gerecht werde ohne des Gesetzes Werke, *allein* durch den Glauben (*Luther Bibel,* 1545).

Even if you cannot read German, you can see here that Luther added the German word *allein* (meaning "alone") into his own German translation. Luther inserted the word *alone* in order to place the false doctrine of "justification by faith alone" into the mouth of the Apostle Paul. However, Saint Paul did not say that a man is justified by faith *alone*. When Martin Luther was confronted about his altered version of Romans 3:28, he retorted, "If your Papist makes much useless fuss about the word *sola* or *allein*, tell him at once: 'Doctor Luther will have it so!'"[26] So much for Luther's defense. Luther fudged the text and the rest is history.

Faith and Works

Still, one might ask why Saint Paul continually insists that we are justified apart from "works of the law." Is this not also implicitly confirming that we are justified by faith alone? To answer this question, we must first discover what Saint Paul meant by "works of the law."

Paul used the phrase "works of the law" six times and only within Romans and Galatians. Here's the full list within context:

1. For no human being will be justified in his sight by **works of the law**, since through the law comes knowledge of sin (Rom 3:20).

2. For we hold that a man is justified by faith apart from **works of law** (Rom 3:28).

3. Yet we know that a man is not justified by **works of the law** but through faith in Jesus Christ, so we also have believed in Christ Jesus, in order to be justified by faith in Christ, and not by works of the law, because by works of the law shall no one be justified (Gal 2:16).

4. Let me ask you only this: Did you receive the Spirit by **works of the law**, or by hearing with faith? (Gal 3:2)

5. Does he who supplies the Spirit to you and works miracles among you do so by **works of the law**, or by hearing with faith? (Gal 3:5)

6. For all who rely on **works of the law** are under a curse. For it is written, 'Cursed be every one who does not abide by all things written in the book of the law, and do them' (Gal 3:10).

When Saint Paul speaks of the "works of the law," he refers to what we know as the six hundred and thirteen precepts of the Torah, such as Jewish prohibitions against eating pork, the mandate of circumcision, and the observance of Passover.

According to Moses, these precepts of the Old Law fall into three divisions: "the precepts, the ceremonies, and the judgments" (Deut 6:1). Saint Thomas Aquinas and the Christian tradition recognize Moses' threefold division as (1) the moral precepts, (2) the ceremonial precepts, and (3) the judicial precepts of the Old Law of Moses.[27]

First, the moral precepts are those precepts known to us as the Ten Commandments—the basic moral law of God for men. Second, the ceremonial precepts relate to such things as the Jewish teaching regarding circumcision on the eighth day and the kosher prohibition against eating pork. Third, the judicial precepts are the civil laws governing the nation of Israel as a political state.

Saint Paul's epistles to the Romans and to the Galatians are particularly concerned with baptized Christians who wrongly believed that the observance of the circumcision and the other *ceremonial* precepts were necessary for salvation. Some Roman and Galatian Christians had wrongly concluded that a Christian must believe in Jesus *and* obey the ceremonial precepts of Moses in order to be saved. Against this error, Saint Paul presents faith in Christ as opposed to the "works of the law." In his historical context, Saint Paul rejected any attempt to bind Christians to the ceremonial law. In other words, Paul did not believe that Christians should receive circumcision or abstain from pork.

What are Works of the Law?

So then, when Saint Paul wrote: "Man is justified by faith apart from works of the law," did he simply mean that Christians are not justified by the ceremonial law? Or did Paul mean that Christians are not justified by works of any sort? To put the question another way, when Saint Paul refers to "works of the law" did he mean "works of the ceremonial law," or did he mean "all works without distinction"? The way we answer this important question determines how we understand "works" with regard to grace and faith.

It would seem that contemporary Protestant scholars associated with the so-called "New Perspective on Paul," such as E.P. Sanders and James Dunn, tend to interpret the "works of the law" as simply referring to circumcision and the ceremonial law.[28] Amateur Catholic apologists also appeal to this interpretation in order to shake off their Protestant interlocutors. Their argument goes something like this: "When Paul writes that a man is justified *by faith apart from works of the law*, he means that a man is justified apart from keeping the *ceremonial law required by Jewish circumcision*. Paul is not arguing against works in general but against Jewish ceremonial works."

This explanation conveniently protects the role of the moral law and faith within justification—something universally affirmed by the Catholic Church.

Notably, Saint Jerome defended this interpretation of "works of the law" as merely the ceremonial precepts of the Old Law. Certainly, within Saint Paul's immediate historical context, he is concerned chiefly with the ceremonial precepts of Moses. We know this because Saint Paul taught that the Gentile Christians should *not* keep the ceremonial precepts of Judaism—they were not to be circumcised and they were not restricted by the Jewish calendar or Jewish dietary regulations.

Nevertheless, Saint Paul includes the moral precepts (for example, "thou shalt not covet") as belonging to the "works of the law" (Rom 7:6-8). Consequently, the Catholic Church has officially followed the interpretation of Saint Augustine, who taught that the phrase "works of the law" refers to the *entire* Law of Moses—to the moral precepts, to the ceremonial precepts, as well as to the judicial precepts. Augustine recognized the "works of the law" referred specifically to the ceremonial precepts in their Jewish context, but he also understood that the message extended to a general interpretation of "works."

Corresponding to this Augustinian tradition, the Catholic Church, at the Council of Trent, declared with Paul that none of the works of the law could justify a man:

> CANON I. If any one says that man may be justified before God *by his own works*, whether done through the teaching of human nature*, or that of the law, without the grace of God through Jesus Christ*—let him be anathema.[29]

This canon from the Council of Trent demonstrates that the Catholic Church does not distinguish between "works" and "works of the law" when stating that a man is not justified by "works of the law." Instead, the

Catholic Church condemns anyone who attempts to justify himself "by his own works," regardless of whether the works belong to the moral precepts or to the ceremonial precepts of the law. Hence, one cannot be justified even if he perfectly fulfilled the moral precepts of the Ten Commandments, since these do not equip a man for the beatific vision of God's essence. The ceremonial precepts ("do not eat swine's flesh") cannot transform us into the righteousness of Christ. Moreover, not even obedience to the moral precepts ("thou shalt not kill") can fill us with the Holy Spirit. The Council of Trent elaborates:

> We are therefore said to be justified freely, because that none of those things which precede justification—whether faith or works—merit the grace itself of justification. For, if it be a grace, it is not now by works, otherwise, as the same Apostle says, grace is no more grace.[30]

Grace remains primary in Catholic teaching. Neither faith nor works merit our justification. Justification is received by faith and perfected by works of charity, but it is not earned by works alone. Yes, prevenient grace is needed even for our initial faith in Christ. No man can be justified simply by observing the moral law found in the Ten Commandments. This is the authentic Catholic teaching of the Catholic Church. "And without faith it is impossible to please God" (Heb 11:6). There is a synergy between faith and works, as James teaches (Jas 2:24). It is not faith alone. It is not works alone. It is faith first and works following—each flowing from the wellspring of grace springing from the wounded side of the crucified Christ.

We would be wrong to assume that Saint Paul taught that the moral precepts of the Ten

Commandments no longer applied to Christians. "Do we then overthrow the law by this faith? By no means! On the contrary, we uphold the law" (Rom 3:31). We have already established how Saint Paul teaches that good works in themselves cannot justify the sinner. However, this does not entail that works have no role in our salvation. Many Protestants wrongly believe that Catholics hold to *justification by works alone* since we do not believe in *justification by faith alone*. For the Catholic, works without faithful love are worthless. The Catholic does not believe that one must choose between *either* faith *or* works. Instead, the Catholic Church exhorts her children to *both* faith *and* works. Saint Paul confirms that faith *alone* is not enough:

> If I have all faith, so as to remove mountains, but have not love, I am nothing. If I give away all I have, and if I deliver my body to be burned, but have not love, I gain nothing (1 Cor 13:2-3).

Faith cannot be alone because it must be accompanied by love. Moreover, love is not passive but active. Love works. Love operates. Saint Paul summed up the Catholic doctrine of justification perfectly in Galatians when he wrote, "For in Christ Jesus neither circumcision nor uncircumcision is of any avail, but faith working through love" (Gal 5:6). Faith working through love. This is the Catholic doctrine of justification. Faith in Christ must be informed by love for Christ. This is a working faith. As our Lord Jesus Christ explained, "If you love me, you will keep my commandments" (Jn 14:15). A faith that is opposed to obedience is a faith without love. It is not saving faith.

Justification: Being Made Righteous

Martin Luther's Protestant mistranslation of Romans 3:28 as "justification by faith *alone*" relates to his error that justification means that a sinner is merely "declared righteous." The Catholic Church instead teaches that justification entails that sinners are "made righteous" in Christ. The Latin *iustificare* arises from a combination of the Latin word for "righteous" {*iustus*} and the Latin verb "to make" {*facere*}—hence, "to make righteous." This conforms to Saint Paul's use of the Greek verb δικαιόω (pronounced *dikaioo*) for the justification of a sinner, since the Greek verb *dikaioo* literally means "make righteous," not merely "declare righteous." Even Protestant scholars such as Philip Schaff have admitted that Greek verbs ending with όω should be translated as an actual manifestation of the actions they describe.[31] Hence, δικαιόω means "make righteous" on account of the verbal ending όω, which denotes a process of making or production. The Catholic emphasis on being *made righteous* refers to the Pauline doctrine that Christ transforms the sinner into a new creation.

The meaning of the word "justification" may seem like an incidental point, but it birthed a highly charged debate at the time of the Reformation. Martin Luther and John Calvin claimed that justification did not *make* us inherently righteous.[32] For these Protestants, justification referred to the imputation or declaration of righteousness. By this, they meant that the righteousness of Christ was credited to us—they denied that believers actually become inherently righteous.

Luther infamously taught that the justified Christian is like animal manure covered with snow. Luther writes:

> I said before that our righteousness is dung in the sight of God. Now if God chooses to adorn dung, he can therefore do it.[33]

There is one passage in particular that demonstrates the errors of Luther's doctrine of justification. Unfortunately, the passage is so obscene and explicit that I feel uncomfortable reproducing it in the text of this book. Nevertheless, I decided to include the quotation because it demonstrates the destructive nature of Luther's heretical theology. However, I have moved his quote to an endnote at the end of this chapter[34] so that readers need not read profane words in the midst of a book about Saint Paul. Let it suffice to say that Luther identified Christians with excrement.

Dung is inherently stinky, vile, and repulsive. However, when cold snow falls upon the excrement, it limits the smell and hides it from sight. Likewise, said Luther, a Christian is a malodorous sinner in God's presence. In Luther's account, when the sinner is justified, Christ covers him like snow so that his repulsive characteristics are hidden in God's sight. We sinners become covered and hidden on the outside, but we remain inwardly disgusting. In other words, Luther understood righteousness as something extrinsic rather than as something intrinsic. Exterior and credited—not interior and inherent. Regrettably, Luther's doctrine of fecal justification denied every means of grace in the Catholic Church:

> And let us tread underfoot and utterly abhor, as a polluted garment and the deadly poison of the devil, all the power of free will, all the wisdom and righteousness of the world, all religious orders, all Masses, ceremonies, vows, fasts, hair shirts, and the like.[35]

The Catholic Church resolutely rejected this extrinsic articulation of justification. According to the Catholic Church, the justified Christian is not merely covered over by Christ. Rather, the sinner is transformed by Christ progressively until he becomes fully righteous—a saint of God.

It is true that Paul speaks of "putting on Christ" (Rom 13:14), but this image need not be interpreted as strictly extrinsic. For example, we "put on" lotion so that it enters our body and heals our skin. The biblical motif of anointing as it regards the *Messiah* (Hebrew for "anointed") or *Christ* (Greek for "anointed") lends itself to an intrinsic interpretation. Anointing with oil is a beautiful illustration of how an exterior reality is absorbed into the inner man.

One can see how Luther's fecal version of justification easily lends itself to "faith alone," since he believed that works could never transform excrement into anything other than excrement. However, the Catholic Church holds that faith and works progressively transform the justified person into the righteousness of Christ. Saint Paul explicitly confirms this Catholic teaching of transformative justification:

> For our sake he made Him to be sin who knew no sin, so that in Him we might *become the righteousness of God* (2 Cor 5:21).

Here Paul states that justification involves a person *becoming* righteous—not merely being covered over or declared righteous. This verse overturns everything Luther and Calvin taught regarding their false doctrine of justification as "being declared righteous." Some Protestants reply that Paul's phrase "we might *become the righteousness of God*" (2 Cor 5:21) describes the Apostles and their ministry—not the justification of sinners. A

Protestant is required to reinterpret the verse this way, since the obvious interpretation undermines the Protestant doctrine of faith alone and justification by imputation.

While the passage does refer to the Apostles in their ministry of reconciliation, the phrase "that in Him we might become the righteousness of God" (2 Cor 5:21) cannot be limited to the Apostles. If we limited the phrase "that in Him we might become the righteousness of God" to only the Apostles, it would imply that being an Apostle makes one righteous. If that were the case, then the Apostle named Judas Iscariot would have been a great saint regardless of his actions. Obviously, this was not the case. Instead, the best way to interpret the passage is the literal way: In Christ we actually *become* righteous. Becoming righteous entails a Catholic process of sanctification—not the Lutheran doctrine of being declared righteous in view of Christ.

Saint Paul further confirms Catholicism's doctrine of transformative justification when he writes:

> For those whom he foreknew he also predestined *to be conformed to the image of his Son*, in order that he might be the first-born among many brethren (Rom 8:29).

The predestined plan of God is that believers might "be conformed to the image of his Son." God does not desire human fecal matter to be hidden under snow or to be sealed off in Ziploc baggies. Instead, he desires to *transform* what is ugly into what is beautiful—what is repulsive into what is desirable—sinners into saints.

The Three Justifications of Abraham

If we read Saint Paul's epistle to the Romans, the epistle to the Hebrews, and the epistle of Saint James together as a symphonic account of Abraham's life, we discover that Abraham was "justified" at *least three times:*

 i. Genesis 12: Abraham responds to God's call and leaves his fatherland.
 ii. Genesis 15: Abraham believes God's promise to make him the exalted father of many nations.
 iii. Genesis 22: Abraham obeys God's command to sacrifice Isaac on Mount Moriah—an act interrupted by the agency of an angel.

Abraham's justification occurs as an initial event accompanied by several subsequent justifications. In Scripture, justification is by no means limited to a single past event in the life of Abraham or in the life of any other believer. Rather, we can speak of the tenses of justification as past, present, and future. We have been justified, we are being justified, and we will be justified at the final judgment of Christ. The unfolding of justification over time reveals the proper relationship between faith and works in the justification of the believer.

The First Justification of Abraham—Gen 12

Genesis 12 recounts how Abraham trusted God's promises and left his homeland in search for the Promised Land of God. The epistle to the Hebrews refers to the virtue of Abraham's faith when he left his homeland:

> By faith he that is called Abraham, obeyed to go
> out into a place which he was to receive for an
> inheritance, and he went out not knowing where
> he went (Heb 11:8).

Hebrews records that Abraham's faith in Genesis 12 is
an example of the faith that "pleases God." Moreover,
Hebrews 11:10 states that Abraham's faith in Genesis
12 arose from his conviction that he would receive a
"city without foundations and whose architect and
builder was God." Abraham became a believer at this
point and thereby was justified—made righteous—by
God.

The Second Justification of Abraham—Gen 15

The second justification of Abraham occurs in Genesis
15 when Abraham trusts the promise of God regarding
the descendents of Abraham through Isaac. Abraham's
faith in this promise in Genesis 15 is the centerpiece of
Paul's discussion of justification. In Romans 4, the
Apostle employs the example of Abraham's faith in this
special promise of God as his chief paradigm of
justification by faith:

> That is why it depends on faith, in order that the
> promise may rest on grace and be guaranteed to
> all his descendants—not only to the adherents
> of the law but also to those who share the faith
> of Abraham, for he is the father of us all (Rom
> 4:16).

Here, once again, Abraham places his faith in God and
is justified.

> For what does the Scripture say? "Abraham
> believed God, and it was reputed to him unto
> justice" (Rom 4:3).[36]

This event occurred after Abraham's act of faith in
Genesis 12, commemorated in Hebrews 11. We see,
then, that Abraham's justification unfolds as his faith
increases—so that he is "the father of us all" who have
faith.

The Third Justification of Abraham—Gen 22

The third recorded justification of Abraham is the one
described by Saint James. This is the controversial one,
because Saint James specifically claims that Abraham
was "justified by works":

> Was not Abraham our father justified by works,
> when he offered his son Isaac upon the altar?
> You see that faith cooperated {*synergei*} with his
> works, and faith was made perfect {*eteleiothe*} by
> works, and the Scripture was fulfilled {*eplerothe*}
> which says, "Abraham believed God, and it was
> reckoned to him as righteousness" and he was
> called the friend of God. You see that a man is
> justified by works and not by faith alone (Jas
> 2:21-24).

Saint James describes Abraham's obedience in
attempting to sacrifice Isaac in Genesis 22 as
"justification." Protestants, such as John Calvin, attempt
to make little of this passage by claiming that the
justification of Abraham in Genesis 22 was merely a
"proof of justification," whereas Genesis 15 was a true
justification before God.[37] The Scriptures, however, do
not support this conclusion. Note well the language of
Saint James in this passage. I included some of the

Greek to make the message more obvious. Saint James says that the justification of Abraham in Genesis 15 was *fulfilled* {Greek: *eplerothe*} by the justification of Abraham in Genesis 22. The justification of Abraham in Genesis 15 was not a distinct "justification before God" on the one hand, and that in Genesis 22 a "justification before man" on the other hand. Rather, the latter justification is a *fulfillment* of the former. The two justifications are intimately connected.

Moreover, the justification of Abraham in Genesis 22 is a "re-justification" entailing the cooperation or synergy of faith and works. Faith "cooperated" {*synergei*} with works so that his faith "became perfect" {*eteleiothe*} by works. What was the means by which his faith was perfected? It was *works*. Here, works play an instrumental role in human justification.

Abraham is not passing from spiritual death to spiritual life again. That had already happened previously in Genesis 12 and 15. Nevertheless, Saint James identifies the events of Genesis 22 as "justification," in that Abraham was "made righteous." As in the previous justifications of Abraham, this justification is the increase in righteousness that Abraham obtained in his initial justification when he first placed his faith in God in Genesis 12.

A plain reading indicates that the faith of Abraham originated in Genesis 12 and continued throughout his life as evidenced by his hope in the promises of God and his loving obedience to the guidance of God. This faith began in Genesis 12 and yet Abraham was justified in Genesis 15 and again in Genesis 22. The plain reading of these passages reveals that justification is repeatable and progressive—two doctrines that Protestantism rejects. We will discuss this repeatable aspect of justification in the next two chapters as we examine Paul's doctrine of falling from grace.

The Council of Trent: "The Just Being Justified Still"

We have discovered that Scripture never teaches that we are justified by faith *alone*. Moreover, we have seen how works of the law—both moral and ceremonial—do not justify us, since God's grace is necessary for human salvation. We have also observed in the life of Abraham that justification unfolded over time through the cooperation or synergy of faith and works. Besides these three examples in the life of Abraham, the Council of Trent quotes several passages of Sacred Scripture to prove that justification continues in a progressive manner in the life of the believer. Note how the Council Fathers at Trent weave together so many beautiful passages of Scripture into a coherent teaching on justification:

> Having, therefore, been thus justified, and made the friends and domestics of God, advancing from virtue to virtue, "they are renewed day by day" (2 Cor 4:16), as the Apostle says, "by mortifying the members of their own flesh, and by presenting them as instruments of justice" (Rom 6:13) unto sanctification, they, through the observance of the commandments of God and of the Church, "faith cooperating with good works" (Jas 2:22) they increase in this justice which they have received through the grace of Christ, and are further justified, as it is written:
>
> "He that is just, let him be justified still" (Rev 22:11), and again: "Be not afraid to be justified even to death" (Sirach 18:22), and again: "You

> see, that by works a man is justified and not by
> faith alone" (Jas 2:24).
>
> And this increase of justification is what the
> Holy Church begs for when she prays, "Give
> unto us, O Lord, an increase of faith, hope, and
> charity."[38]

Following the Scriptural witnesses to the life of
Abraham, the Catholic Church affirms there is an
"increase of justification," and that increase occurs by
the cooperation of faith *and* works. The Scriptural
evidence proves that justification is like the story of a
soul—it has a beginning, middle, and end. Justification
is not a formal and completed event at the beginning of
salvation. Otherwise, Saint Paul could not speak of how
we "will be justified" (Rom 2:13) in the future. Rather,
justification is something progressive and repeatable.
Moreover, the Church and Saint Augustine teach that
justification can be lost and regained. These quotes from
Saint Paul and Saint Augustine regarding to the loss of
salvation will be explored in CHAPTER FIVE. Before
turning to this subject, however, we must first examine
Paul's teaching on initial justification by faith through
the instrument of baptism in the next chapter.

For the sake of simplicity, below are five
summarizing points regarding the Catholic doctrine of
justification.

Catholic Teaching on Justification in Five Points

1. Faith *alone* does not justify us. Scripture never
   speaks this way.
2. We are not justified by works alone—we cannot
   become perfectly righteous by observing the
   moral precepts nor by observing the ceremonial
   precepts of the Law.

3. Justification entails being *made* righteous—not merely being *declared* righteous—as stated by Paul in 2 Corinthians 5:21.
4. Justification begins with God's grace and progresses through the synergy or cooperation of faith and works.
5. Abraham experienced justification more than once—thereby revealing that justification entails works and an increase in righteousness—as taught by Saint Paul and explained at the Council of Trent.

NOTES

[24] *Luther's Works* 35, 362; 34, 317. "Jimmy" here is an impertinent reference to the inspired epistle of Saint James.

[25] *Luther's Works* 54, 424.

[26] *Luther's Works* 13, 66.

[27] Saint Thomas Aquinas, *Summa theologiae* I-II, q. 99, a. 4.

[28] See especially James Dunn and Alan Suggate's *The Justice of God: A Fresh Look at the Old Doctrine of Justification by Faith* (Grand Rapids: Eerdmans Publishing, 1993).

[29] *Council of Trent,* Session Six, Canon One.

[30] *Council of Trent,* Session Six, Chapter Eight.

[31] Philip Schaff wrote: "Modern exegesis has justified this view of δικαιοω and δικαιωσις according to Hellenestic usage, although etymologically the verb may mean *to make just*, i.e. to sanctify, in accordance with verbs in όω (e.g. δηλοω, φανεροω,

NOTES CONTINUED

τυφοω, *to make* manfest). Philip Schaff, *History of the Christian Church*, Vol 7, f. 2, p. 123.

[32] John Calvin, *Institutes of the Christian Religion* Book 3, Chapter 11. Translated by Ford Lewis Battles. John T. McNeill, ed. Westminster John Knox, 2006.

[33] *Luther's Works*, 34, 184. I am especially grateful to David Armstrong for his assistance in unearthing these quotes from Luther's corpus.

[34] In a most obscene manner, Luther expressed his doctrine of fecal justification in this way: "I am ripe shit, and the world a gigantic asshole; then shall we soon part." *Luther's Works* 54, 448. Luther thought of the justified sinner as a turd. Found also in Richard Marius, *Martin Luther: The Christian Between God and Death* (Harvard University Press, 2000) p. 20.

[35] *Luther's Works*, 26, 41. Translated by Jaroslav Pelikan.

[36] The Catholic Vulgate renders Paul's use of the Greek word λογίζομαι (usually translated as "reckoned") as "reputed." For example: "Credidit Abraham Deo, et *reputatam* est illi ad justitiam" (Rom 4:3, *Clementine Vulgate*). The Protestant might seek to interpret "reputatam" as approximating Luther's version of "imputation," since both "repute" and "impute" derive from the Latin word *putare,* meaning "to think." Yet, this is strained since *imputare* means "charge" or "ascribe," whereas *reputare* means, "think over, reflect." This is why Martin Luther rejected the Vulgate rendering of *reputare* and popularized the rending of *imputare*. The ancient Catholic translation of *reputare* going back to the fourth century demonstrates that God does not merely *declare* us as righteous, but that he

NOTES CONTINUED

counts us as righteous because it is true of us—Christ's righteousness is *in* us not merely credited to us.

[37] John Calvin, *Commentary on the Epistle of James*, Translated by John Owen, at 2:21. "We have already said that James does not speak here of the cause of justification, or of the manner how men obtain righteousness, and this is plain to every one; but that his object was only to shew that good works are always connected with faith; and, therefore, since he declares that Abraham was justified by works, he is speaking of the proof he gave of his justification."

[38] *Council of Trent,* Session 6, Chapter 10.

4. PAUL ON BAPTISM & REGENERATION

> ...all who have been baptized into Christ Jesus
> were baptized into his death...
> ROMANS 6:3

Baptism as Being Born Again

ARE YOU A BORN AGAIN CHRISTIAN? Perhaps you have been asked this question by a neighbor or by someone sitting next to you on an airplane. Usually, the person asking the question assumes that being "born again" is the same thing as "believing that Jesus Christ is your personal Lord and Savior." However, the term "born again" or "regeneration" occurs only three times in the Holy Bible. If we are going to fully appreciate the meaning of "born again," then we need to examine these three passages. The first and most famous passage about being "born again" comes from the Gospel of John:

> Jesus answered him, "Truly, truly, I say to you, unless one is *born again*, he cannot see the kingdom of God."

> Nicodemus said to him, "How can a man be born when he is old? Can he enter a second time into his mother's womb and be born?"

> Jesus answered, "Truly, truly, I say to you, unless one is *born of water and the Spirit*, he cannot enter the kingdom of God" (Jn 3:3-5).

The second "born again" passage comes from the writings of Saint Paul:

> He saved us, not because of deeds done by us in righteousness, but in virtue of his own mercy, by *the washing of regeneration* and renewal in the Holy Spirit (Titus 3:5).

The third "born again" passage is often neglected. It is found in the Gospel of Matthew:

> Jesus said to them, "Truly, I say to you, *in the regeneration*, when the Son of man shall sit on his glorious throne, you who have followed me will also sit on twelve thrones, judging the twelve tribes of Israel" (Mt 19:28).

The first passage from the Gospel of John and the second passage from Titus seem to be speaking of "born again" or "regeneration" with respect to individual persons. The third passage in Matthew seems to be using "regeneration" in a different way, as regarding the end of the world. This last passage demonstrates that regeneration is not merely a past reality in the life of a Christian, but a future salvific event that shall occur at the end of time.

In the Gospel of John, being "born again" is paralleled with being "born of water and of the Holy Spirit." Likewise, Saint Paul links regeneration with "the washing of regeneration." In both cases, the miracle of regeneration is associated with the "water" and "washing." The reason for this is that baptism is the "sacrament of faith." The Catholic Church follows Christ who associates faith with baptism: "He that believes and is baptized shall be saved" (Mark 16:4). His Apostles confirmed this connection:

> Masters, what must I do, that I may be saved? But they said: Believe in the Lord Jesus, and thou shalt be saved, and thy house. And they preached the word of the Lord to him and to all that were in his house. And he, taking them the same hour of the night, washed their stripes, and himself was baptized, and all his house immediately (Acts 16:30-33).

The Catholic Church does not believe that baptism is a magical ritual that somehow saves a person who does not have faith in Christ. Baptism denotes the beginning of the Christian journey. When a runner registers for a marathon, he is given a registration number to pin to his jogging shirt. This number qualifies the runner for the marathon, but it does not ensure that he will in fact finish the race. As the *Catechism of Trent* explains baptism:

> It is the beginning of the most holy Commandments for this obvious reason, that Baptism is, at it were, the gate through which we enter into the fellowship of Christian life, and begin thenceforward to obey the Commandments."[39]

Baptism gives us access into the life of the Holy Spirit since it is the door opening to the other sacraments. In a previous chapter, we examined how Paul's conversion on the road to Damascus led him to discover that every Christian is a member of Christ. This is the doctrine of participation. In this context, Catholic theology particularly understands our participation in Christ through the seven sacraments instituted by Christ. Sacred Scripture and Sacred Tradition confirm that Christ instituted seven sacraments so "that all these things are sufficiently analogous to that life by which the soul lives to God, we discover in them a reason to account for the number of the Sacraments."[40] The seven sacraments of the Catholic Church are as follows:

BAPTISM (Mt 28:19; Rom 6:3-6)

CONFIRMATION (Acts 8:14-17; Heb 6:2)

EUCHARIST (1 Cor 11:24-25)

PENANCE (2 Cor 5:18, Jn 20:21-23)

EXTREME UNCTION (Mk 6:13, Jas 5:14-15)

HOLY ORDERS (Acts 6:3-6; 1 Tim 3:1-9; 4:14-16; 5:17-22)

MATRIMONY (Mt 19:10-11; Eph 5:31-32)

As the initial sacrament of faith, holy baptism is the "ordinary means" by which Jesus Christ grants us the grace of justification. Here the term "ordinary means" means that baptism is the usual or *ordinary* way in which God saves sinners. Our Lord Jesus Christ has covenantally bound Himself to His sacraments, but He is not bound by His sacraments. He can confer justification to a person who desires baptism but dies prior to receiving it. This is what the Church calls *baptismus flaminis* or "baptism by desire." Saint Alphonsus Liguori explained that baptism of water {*baptismus fluminis*, meaning "river baptism"} is to be distinguished from baptism of desire {*baptismus flaminis*, meaning "wind baptism"}.[41] As Saint Thomas Aquinas teaches:

> Man receives the forgiveness of sins before baptism in so far as he has baptism of desire, *explicitly or implicitly;* and yet when he actually receives baptism, he receives a fuller remission, as to the remission of the entire punishment. So also before baptism, Cornelius (Acts 10:1-31) and others like him receive grace and virtues through their faith in Christ and their desire for baptism, implicit or explicit: but afterwards when baptized, they receive a yet greater fullness of grace and virtues.[42]

So then, justification is ordinarily bound to baptism as the sacrament of faith since we are justified by faith as Paul taught. This is why the Council of Trent identifies baptism as the instrumental cause of baptism. Baptism is the instrument by which God justifies us. Just as a violinist might use a violin to play a piece of music, the violin accomplishes the task *only because it is held in the hand of a talented musician.* So also, "baptism saves us" (1 Pet 3:21) because it is Christ's divinely appointed means for salvation—and it is Christ who mystically ministers at every single valid baptism. When we appreciate the instrumental role of baptism in Catholic theology, we can also appreciate how the Council of Trent clarified the doctrine of justification by delineating the "five causes of justification." The Sixth Session of the Council of Trent explains the mechanics of justification and the sacraments in the following way:

> Of this Justification the Causes are these:

i. the final cause indeed is the glory of God and of Jesus Christ, and life everlasting;

ii. the efficient cause is a merciful God who washes and sanctifies gratuitously, signing, and anointing with the Holy Spirit of promise, who is the pledge of our inheritance;

iii. the meritorious cause is His most beloved only-begotten, our Lord Jesus Christ, who, when we were enemies, for the exceeding charity wherewith he loved us, merited Justification for us by His most holy Passion on the wood of the cross, and made satisfaction for us unto God the Father;

iv. the instrumental cause is the sacrament of baptism, which is the sacrament of faith, without which faith no man was ever justified;

v. lastly, the alone formal cause is the justice of God, not that whereby He Himself is just, but that whereby He maketh us just, that, to wit, with which we being endowed by Him, are renewed in the spirit of our mind, and we are not only reputed, but are truly called, and are, just, receiving justice within us, each one according to his own measure, which the Holy Ghost distributes to every one as He wills, and according to each one's proper disposition and co-operation.[43]

Here we have a very helpful description of the role of baptism and of Christ's merits in human salvation. We also learn that justification is entirely gratuitous.

If, however, salvation is a gift, one might ask, why is it attached to a water ritual? We find in the First Epistle of Peter the stunning words "baptism now saves you" (1 Pet 3:21). In this context, Peter relates baptism to the flood in which Noah and his family were saved. Baptism, says Peter, is the antitype or fulfillment of this miraculous deliverance. Just as the waters of the flood cleansed the earth of sin and corruption, so also does Christ use baptism to cleanse the soul and pour out His Holy Spirit. As Peter proclaimed at Pentecost, "Repent, and be baptized every one of you in the name of Jesus Christ for the forgiveness of your sins; and you shall receive the gift of the Holy Spirit" (Acts 2:38). We find Ananias saying something similar to Paul when he was baptized in Damascus: "And now why do you wait? Rise and be baptized, and wash away your sins, calling on His name" (Acts 22:16).

Saint Paul also taught that baptism incorporated us into Christ: "For as many of you as were baptized into Christ have put on Christ" (Gal 3:27). Baptism unites the believer to both the death and resurrection of Christ:

> Do you not know that all of us who have been baptized into Christ Jesus were baptized into his death? We were buried therefore with him by baptism into death, so that as Christ was raised from the dead by the glory of the Father, we too might walk in newness of life. For if we have been united with him in a death like his, we shall certainly be united with him in a resurrection like his. We know that our old self was crucified with him so that the sinful body might be

destroyed, and we might no longer be enslaved to sin (Rom 6:3-6).

Everyone who has been baptized has been baptized into the death of Christ. It could not be explained any more clearly. Baptism "buries" us into the death of Christ so that we can be "united with him in a resurrection like his."

A striking feature of Romans 6:3-6 is that by being united to Christ, baptism also liberates us from "the sinful body" that is "enslaved to sin." Here Saint Paul refers to the doctrine of original sin. Saint Paul would no doubt have been familiar with the Psalm that states, "Behold, I was brought forth in iniquity, and in sin did my mother conceive me" (Ps 51:5). Paul would later articulate the doctrine of original sin more fully. In fact, the Catholic Church looks back to the Apostle for its formulation of original sin as applying to every human person born after Adam:

> If any one asserts, that the prevarication of Adam injured himself alone, and not his posterity; and that the holiness and justice, received of God, which he lost, he lost for himself alone, and not for us also; or that he, being defiled by the sin of disobedience, has only transfused death, and pains of the body, into the whole human race, but not sin also, which is the death of the soul; let him be anathema—whereas he contradicts the Apostle Paul who says: "By one man sin entered into the world, and by sin death, and so death passed upon all men, in whom all have sinned."[44]

Saint Paul further describes the universal application of original sin to the Christians of Corinth:

> For as by a man came death, by a man has come
> also the resurrection of the dead. For as in
> Adam all die, so also in Christ shall all be made
> alive (1 Cor 15:21-22).

In Adam, all people die. Adam and Eve transmitted to
their descendants human nature wounded by their own
first sin. We are not born in a state of grace. Rather, we
have been deprived of original holiness and justice, and
this deprivation is called original sin. The scope of this
deprivation, unfortunately, also includes infants.

> By reason of this rule of faith, from a tradition
> of the Apostles, even infants, who could not as
> yet commit any sin of themselves, are for this
> cause truly baptized for the remission of sins,
> that in them that may be cleansed away by
> regeneration, which they have contracted by
> generation. For, unless a man be born again of
> water and the Holy Ghost, he cannot enter into
> the kingdom of God.[45]

Infant Baptism

We learn that the grace of justification and
sanctification, as it relies on faith in Christ, is conjoined
with baptism as the sacrament of faith. Saint Paul
confirms this in his First Epistle to the Corinthians:
"You were washed, you were sanctified, you were
justified in the name of the Lord Jesus Christ and in the
Spirit of our God" (1 Cor 6:11). Since children are
conceived with original sin, it comes as no surprise that
Christians have baptized infants from the very first days
of the Church. We find evidence of infant baptism in
the New Testament and in the writings of the early
Christians.

However, the precedent for infant baptism actually goes back further than the New Testament and resides in the Old Testament. God commanded Abraham to place the "sign of the covenant" upon himself and upon his children, even his newborn infants:

> You shall be circumcised in the flesh of your foreskins, and it shall be a sign of the covenant between me and you. He that is eight days old among you shall be circumcised (Gen 17:11-12).

Saint Paul tells us that circumcision was for Abraham and his children "a sign or seal of the righteousness which he had by faith" (Rom 4:11). In other words, circumcision was a kind of "sacrament of faith" in the Old Testament. As Thomas Aquinas explained: "It is manifest that circumcision was a preparation for Baptism."[46] The notion that circumcision is somehow the Old Testament type of New Testament baptism is also found in the writings of Saint Paul. The Apostle wrote to the Christians in Colossae, reminding them of how they did not need to be circumcised, because they had instead been baptized:

> In Him also you were circumcised with a circumcision made without hands, by putting off the body of flesh in the circumcision of Christ; and you were buried with him in baptism, in which you were also raised with him through faith in the working of God, who raised him from the dead (Col 2:11-12).

Saint Paul relates that baptism rendered the Colossian Christians as spiritually circumcised. Hence, Paul clearly perceived the covenantal connection between circumcision and baptism.

It follows, then, that if circumcision had been administered to infants, then baptism should likewise be administered to infants. This is precisely what we find in the New Testament.

> And Peter said to them, "Repent, and be baptized every one of you in the name of Jesus Christ for the forgiveness of your sins; and you shall receive the gift of the Holy Spirit. *For the promise is to you and to your children*" (Acts 2:38-39).

We also know that it was Saint Paul's custom to baptize entire households, following the covenantal model of household circumcision in the Old Testament. We read in the Acts of the Apostles that when Saint Paul preached in the city of Philippi, a certain woman named Lydia heard the Gospel of Jesus Christ. "The Lord opened her heart to give heed to what was said by Paul. And she was baptized, with her household" (Acts 16:14-15). In Jewish culture, as well as in Greco-Roman societies, the domestic household included spouses, children, relatives, and sometimes servants.

In the same chapter in the Acts of the Apostles, we read about the Philippian jailor who underwent a conversion through the instruction of Saint Paul. The jailor "was baptized at once, with all his family" (Acts 16:33). The same thing occurs when Paul came to Corinth:

> Crispus, the ruler of the synagogue, believed in the Lord, together with his entire household; and many of the Corinthians hearing Paul believed and were baptized (Acts 18:8).

Furthermore, Paul himself explains that it was his custom to baptize not only adults, but also entire households: "I did baptize also the household of Stephanas" (1 Cor 1:16). Paul's custom of baptizing families corresponded to the universal promise given to Abraham: "And in your posterity shall *all the families* of the earth be blessed" (Acts 3:25). Appealing to Saint Paul's practice of household baptism, the Catholic Church finds support for the practice of baptizing infants for the remission of original sin:

> That this law extends not only to adults but also to infants and children, and that the Church has received this form Apostolic Tradition, is confirmed by the unanimous teaching and authority of the Fathers.[47]

Writing in about A.D. 215, Saint Hippolytus wrote: "Baptize first the children, and if they can speak for themselves let them do so. Otherwise, let their parents or other relatives speak for them."[48] Similarly, Saint Augustine wrote:

> The custom of Mother Church in baptizing infants is certainly not to be scorned, nor is it to be regarded in any way as superfluous, nor is it to be believed that its tradition is anything except apostolic.[49]

The Sacrament of Confirmation

Related to the sacrament of baptism is the sacrament of confirmation. Saint Cyprian of Carthage, writing in about A.D. 253, explained the need for this post-baptismal sacrament:

> It is necessary for him that has been baptized also to be anointed, so that by his having received chrism, that is, the anointing, he can be the anointed of God and have in him the grace of Christ.[50]

This sacramental anointing is called "confirmation" from the Latin *confirmatio,* meaning "making firm or strong." The earliest Popes affirmed this sacrament:

> That in Confirmation is contained the true and proper nature of a Sacrament has always been acknowledged by the Catholic Church, as Pope Melchiades and many other very holy and very ancient Pontiffs expressly declare.[51]

Confirmation consists in the anointing of the head and the laying on of hands by the bishop on those who have already been baptized. We read about this custom in the Acts of the Apostles. After Philip the deacon successfully converted and baptized a community of Samaritans, the apostles Peter and John went to Samaria in order to confer the sacrament of confirmation to the newly baptized believers, "that they might receive the Holy Spirit. For it had not yet fallen on any of them, but they had only been baptized in the name of the Lord Jesus. Then they laid their hands on them and they received the Holy Spirit" (Acts 8:14-17).

When the Apostles laid their hands on those who had been baptized, they received the "completion of baptism." Through the laying on of hands, the baptized were anointed by the Holy Spirit. They were now fully Christian. For this reason, the Catholic Church teaches that the effect of the sacrament of confirmation is the special outpouring of the Holy Spirit as once granted to the apostles "on the day of

Pentecost, so great was the power of the Holy Ghost with which they were all filled."[52] So just as the sacrament of baptism unites us to the death and resurrection of Christ, so the sacrament of confirmation joins us to the mystery of the outpouring of the Holy Spirit on the day of Pentecost.

We also find Saint Paul practicing the sacrament of confirmation:

> On hearing this, they were baptized in the name of the Lord Jesus. Moreover, when Paul had laid his hands upon them, the Holy Spirit came on them (Acts 19:5-6).

We see in these passages that the Apostles distinguished between two unique sacraments. According to the epistle to the Hebrews, instructions "about baptisms and the laying on of hands" are among the "elemental teachings" of the Christian faith (Heb 6:1-2). These two sacraments marked the initiation and further strengthening of the Christian believer. The first was baptism by water, and the second was confirmation through the laying on of hands. We also see that deacons and others could administer baptism, but the power to confirm was restricted to the Apostles. For this reason, only Catholic bishops have the ordinary right to confer the sacrament of confirmation by the laying on of hands and anointing. However, in extraordinary circumstances, a Catholic priest may confer the sacrament of confirmation by administering the holy oil known as sacred chrism which has been previously consecrated by the bishop. When administrating the sacrament of confirmation, the bishop says, "I sign thee with the sign of the cross, I confirm thee with the chrism of salvation, in the name of the Father and of the Son and of the Holy Ghost," or alternatively, "Be sealed with the Gift of the Holy Spirit," because the person receives the seal or mark of the Holy Spirit.

> Besides, that mark by which the Christian is distinguished from all others, as the soldier is by certain badges, should be impressed on the more conspicuous part of the body.[53]

The sacred chrism is a sweet-smelling olive oil that has been mixed with balsam. Those who have received the sacrament of confirmation often recall the sweet smell that accompanied their reception of the sacrament. According to Saint Thomas Aquinas, the Apostle Paul spoke of the sacrament of confirmation in this regard: "For we are the aroma of Christ to God" (2 Cor 2:15).[54] Likewise, the Catholic Church cites this Pauline passage in relation to the sacrament of confirmation:

> Nor indeed could any other matter than that of chrism seem more appropriate to declare the effects of this Sacrament. Oil, by its nature rich, unctuous and fluid, expresses the fullness of grace, which, through the Holy Ghost, overflows and is poured into others from Christ the head, like the ointment that ran down upon the beard of Aaron, to the skirt of his garment; for God anointed him with the oil of gladness, above his fellows, and of his fullness we all have received."[55]

Saint Paul elsewhere speaks of this special "seal" that early Christians had received through the sacrament of confirmation:

> He has put his seal upon us and given us his
> Spirit in our hearts as a guarantee (2 Cor 1:22).

> In him you also, who have heard the word of
> truth, the gospel of your salvation, and have
> believed in him, were sealed with the promised
> Holy Spirit (Eph 1:13).

> And do not grieve the Holy Spirit of God, in
> whom you were sealed for the day of
> redemption (Eph 4:30).

After receiving this seal, the traditional Roman Rite
instructs the bishop to lightly slap the cheek of the
newly confirmed "to make him recollect that, as a
valiant combatant, he should be prepared to endure
with unconquered spirit all adversities for the name of
Christ."[56]

Thus, we have seen how Saint Paul relates
regeneration to the divine grace that we receive in
baptism. We observed the power of baptism as it
overcomes the privation of righteousness that was lost
to us on account of original sin. This explains why Paul
identified circumcision as prefiguring baptism, and how
it was therefore suitable for children and family
households. Lastly, we observed how Saint Paul and the
other Apostles coupled the sacrament of baptism with
the sacrament of confirmation through the laying on of
hands and anointing. Just as baptism corresponds to the
death and resurrection of Christ, so also, the sacrament
of confirmation corresponds to the day of Pentecost
when the Holy Spirit was poured out on the Church.
Confirmation also marks us with the seal of the Holy
Spirit and completes the grace received in baptism.
Having now established the initiation of the Christian
into the Church, we will next examine how Saint Paul

understood the effects of sin in those who neglect the grace of God given to them in baptism. We turn to the sacrament of confession.

NOTES

[39] *Catechism of Trent, 150.*

[40] *Catechism of Trent,* 141.

[41] Saint Alphonsus Liguori, *Moral Theology,* Book 6, nn. 95-7.

[42] Saint Thomas Aquinas, *Summa theologiae* III, q. 69, a. 4.

[43] *Council of Trent,* Session Six, Chapter Seven.

[44] *Council of Trent,* Session Five, Chapter Two.

[45] *Council of Trent,* Session Five, Chapter Four.

[46] Saint Thomas Aquinas, *Summa theologiae* III, q. 70, a. 1.

[47] *Catechism of Trent,* 164.

[48] Saint Hippolytus, *The Apostolic Tradition* 21:16.

[49] Saint Augustine, *The Literal Interpretation of Genesis* 10, 23, 39.

[50] Saint Cyprian of Carthage, *Letters* 7, 2.

[51] *Catechism of Trent,* 184.

[52] *Catechism of Trent,* 194.

[53] *Catechism of Trent,* 195.

[54] Saint Thomas Aquinas, *Summa theologiae* III, q. 72, a. 2.

[55] *Catechism of Trent,* 195.

[56] *Catechism of Trent,* 195.

5. PAUL ON FALLING FROM GRACE & RECONCILIATION

...you have fallen away from grace...
GALATIANS 5:4

Once Saved Always Saved?

MOST EVANGELICAL CHRISTIANS HOLD that a Christian is "once saved always saved," by which they mean that once a person has committed his life to Christ, he can never do anything to undo this gift of salvation. The explanation assumes that since the gift of salvation was freely granted, there is nothing that one can do to lose it. Contrary to this, we know that gifts can be abandoned, rejected, or destroyed by the ill will of the recipient. A father may purchase a sports car and freely give it to his son as a gift. It is rightly assumed that a gift cannot be "ungifted" or taken away. I am sure that the son would receive the car gleefully. However, the son may turn around and sell the car for drugs, crash the car, or neglect the car so that it no longer functions. The gift was not "ungifted." Rather, the worth of the gift was rejected through negligence.

Catholicism views salvation in a similar way—a gift is given freely, but it may be spurned and squandered. The Father freely gave His Son Jesus Christ to suffer, die, and rise again for our salvation. Through the Holy Spirit, God pours out this love upon us so that we become the children of God. In the words of Saint Paul, we become earthen vessels containing inestimable treasure (1 Cor 4:7). And this salvation is a gift. As Saint Paul wrote:

> For by grace you have been saved through faith; and this is not your own doing, it is the gift of God—not because of works, lest any man should boast. For we are his workmanship, created in Christ Jesus for good works, which God prepared beforehand, that we should walk in them (Eph 2:8-10).

This gift of God is not "earned by works of our own doing," but rather is received "through faith." However, notice that salvation has a purpose in this life. We are "created in Christ Jesus *for good works*...that we should walk in them." Paul is opposed to certain persons trying to earn salvation through works *without faith*, but he finds no tension between faith and good works once faith has been established in the Christian. In fact, Paul expects that good works will necessarily grow up as the fruits of faith. Recall that Saint Paul, like the Catholic Church, finds salvation through "faith working through love" and not through "faith alone."

This difference demonstrates that for Saint Paul and the Catholic Church, salvation is understood as progressive and multidimensional. When Evangelicals read Paul, they observe a stress on "faith," and so they focus on this aspect of Paul's teaching. The Catholic Church reads Paul and discovers in his writings a stress on faith, but in the context of various other doctrines: baptism, the church, good works, tradition, liturgy, sanctification, etc. To use an illustration, it is as if two different people look at a written piece of music. The first looks at the piece, and after studying concludes,

"The note D seems to be predominate." Then he walks over to the piano and strikes a D on the piano. The other person studies the same sheet of music and concludes, "This piece of music is in the key of D." He then walks over to the piano and plays the beautiful piece of music from the sheet in the key of D. The first person tried to distill the music down to one note, and as a result, he neglected the rest. However, the second person realized that D was the overarching theme, and yet he incorporated all the other notes so that something more beautiful resulted.

Non-Catholics, in their commendable zeal, often distill the writings of Saint Paul to such an extent that they miss the complexities and nuances of the Apostle. They play one note—faith—and neglect the other notes. This is especially the case when it comes to Saint Paul's doctrine of salvation. As a result, the Evangelical doctrine of "once saved always saved" misses the nuances of Paul's doctrine. Paul does in fact teach that "nothing can separate us from the love of God" (Rom 8:39). However, he also clearly states that certain Christians have "fallen from grace" (Gal 5:4). What does the Apostle mean, then, when he says that certain Christians have fallen from grace?

The Apostle explains, "I beat my body and make it my slave so that after I have preached to others, I myself will not be disqualified for the prize" (1 Cor 9:27). Here the prize is salvation, as is clear from the preceding verses. Saint Paul follows a disciplined life because he knows that there is a possibility that he might forfeit the salvation that he preaches. For this reason, Paul encourages the Christians in Corinth to do the same: "So, if you think you are standing firm, be careful that you do not fall" (1 Cor 10:12). The "fall" here is the "fall from grace" spoken about by Paul in Galatians 5:4. In both verses, Paul uses the same Greek verb for "fall." Interestingly enough, the warning about falling from grace in Galatians 5:4 is immediately followed up by Paul's exhortation to have "faith working through love" in Galatians 5:6. Faith must work. If faith does not work, then it becomes "dead faith"—a faith that does not justify. Notably, Saint Augustine endorsed the view that Christians can fall from grace and thereby lose their justification. Augustine writes:

> If, however, being already regenerate and justified, he relapses of his own will into an evil life, assuredly he cannot say, "I have not received," because of his own free choice to evil he has lost the grace of God, that he had received.[57]

Augustine, like Paul, held that those "already regenerate and justified" could lose the grace of God. He also warned against those who might say that they never received salvation. Let no one be deceived. Augustine taught that the regenerate can lose the grace of God. All Lutherans and Calvinists who claim Augustine should read Augustine on their own and discover that Augustine was not a proto-Protestant.[58] And why did Augustine hold that grace could be lost? Because he was a disciple of Saint Paul's letters. Since the Apostle taught that one might fall from grace, he elsewhere encouraged the Christians in Philippi to "work out your salvation with fear and trembling" (Phil 2:12). Here again we see Paul's emphasis on a "faith working through love" (Gal 5:6).

While salvation is a gift, it requires our effort. If you receive the gift of a bicycle, it is worthless until you actually get on the bike and start peddling. If the giver of the gift saw the bicycle leaning against the wall in your garage covered in dust, he would be offended. The giver wanted the recipient to enjoy cycling, but this intention was never realized. The same is true of salvation. The gift of salvation has been given to us so that we can be conformed to the image of His Son (Rom 8:29). This is a profound honor. We are called not only to believe in Christ, but also to become like Christ. We participate in the life of *Christ*. It is for this reason that we are called *Christians*. This means that our life is characterized by acts pertaining to faith, hope, and charity (1 Cor 13:13). When we willingly break our bond of charity with Christ, we fall from grace.

We learn from Saint John that some sins are "mortal sins" and some sins are not mortal in this way:

> If any one sees his brother committing what is not a mortal sin, he will ask, and God will give him life for those whose sin is not mortal. There is sin that is mortal. I do not say that one is to pray for that. All wrongdoing is sin, but there is sin that is not mortal (1 Jn 5:16-17).

Following John's classification of these two kinds of sins, the Catholic Church teaches the following about mortal sin:

> All mortal sins must be revealed to the priest. Venial sins, which do not separate us from the grace of God, and into which we frequently fall, although they may be usefully confessed, as the experience of the pious proves, may be omitted without sin, and expiated by a variety of other means. Mortal sins, as we have already said, are all to be confessed, even though they be most secret, or be opposed only to the last two Commandments of the Decalogue. Such secret

> sins often inflict deeper wounds on the soul
> than those which are committed openly and
> publicly.[59]

Mortal sins are called "mortal" because, as Saint John explained, they bring death to the soul. The other class is called "venial sin" from the Latin word *venia*, meaning "forgiveness" or "pardon."

Non-Catholics understand the difference between mortal and venial sins whether they acknowledge it or not. For example, if you were playing golf with your pastor and he let out a curse word when he hit his golf ball into the forest, you would be disappointed but not broken-hearted. However, if your pastor were engaged in an adulterous affair with the church's secretary, you would have cause for alarm. The same is true in marriage. There are certain sins that inhibit the growth of love between a husband and wife, but do not rupture the loving relationship, as would adultery or physical abuse. Similarly, some sins are venial sins and some sins are mortal sins.

According to the traditional teaching of the Church, three conditions must be met in order for a sin to be mortal: "Mortal sin is sin whose object is grave matter and which is also committed with full knowledge and deliberate consent."[60] Would Paul agree with this? As a matter of fact, the Catholic Church looks to Paul as the principal delineator of mortal sins. The Apostle's epistle to the Galatians is a classic example of grave sins and their terrible consequence for the soul:

> Now the works of the flesh are plain:
> fornication, impurity, licentiousness, idolatry,
> sorcery, enmity, strife, jealousy, anger,
> selfishness, dissension, party spirit, envy,
> drunkenness, carousing, and the like. I warn you,

as I warned you before, that *those who do such things shall not inherit the kingdom of God* (Gal 5:18-21).

Who is Paul warning? He is warning Christians. If they do these things, then they will fall from grace. In other words, they "shall not inherit the kingdom of God." Paul shows that there are certain sins that are mortal. These sins disqualify a Christian from inheriting the kingdom of God. The Apostle could not explain it any more clearly. In fact, these "mortal sin lists" are a common feature of Paul's epistles. For more examples of Paul's lists of mortal sins, see also Rom 1:28-32; 1 Cor 6:9-10; Eph 5:3-5; Col 3:5-8; 1 Tim 1:9-10; 2 Tim 3:2-5.

We find further confirmation of "falling from grace" when we turn to the epistle to the Hebrews. While the epistle to the Hebrews does not bear the name of Paul, Catholic tradition has held it to be "Pauline" in origin. Some have speculated that its core was by Paul and that it was later composed and polished by Saint Luke on behalf of Paul. Others believe that it lacks the signature of Paul because it is addressed to the Hebrews. This makes sense when we remember that Paul was the Apostle to the Gentiles. Whichever the reason, the epistle certainly incorporates the theology of Paul and resembles the epistle to the Galatians in many ways.

In the epistle to the Hebrews, we find three passages that echo the exhortations found in the other epistles of Paul about falling from grace. In Hebrews 4:1 we read, "The promise of entering his rest still stands, let us be careful that none of you be found to have fallen short of it." Here, the assumption is that a Christian may "fall short" of entering into heaven. Hebrews 6:4-6 is a difficult passage for Evangelicals and is often admitted to be the one passage that refutes the Evangelical doctrine of "once saved always saved."

> For it is impossible to restore again to repentance those who have once been enlightened, who have tasted the heavenly gift, and have become partakers of the Holy Spirit, and have tasted the goodness of the word of God and the powers of the age to come, if they then commit apostasy, since they crucify the Son of God on their own account and hold him up to contempt (Heb 6:4-6).

Here we have persons who have been "enlightened, who have tasted the heavenly gift, and have become partakers of the Holy Spirit," and yet they are able to "commit apostasy" and reject the Son of God. Two verses later, he compares such apostates to thistles worthy only of being burned (Heb 6:8).

The epistle to the Hebrews later takes up the problem of apostate Christians in its tenth chapter. It is worth quoting in full.

> For if we sin deliberately after receiving the knowledge of the truth, there no longer remains a sacrifice for sins, but a fearful prospect of judgment, and a fury of fire that will consume the adversaries. A man who has violated the Law of Moses dies without mercy at the testimony of two or three witnesses. How much worse punishment do you think will be deserved by *the man who has spurned the Son of God, and profaned the blood of the covenant by which he was sanctified, and outraged the Spirit of grace?* For we know him who said, "Vengeance is mine, I will repay." Again, "The Lord will judge his people."

> It is a fearful thing to fall into the hands of the
> living God (Heb 10:26-31).

This passage confirms Paul's doctrine of apostasy and
the warning set forth in the sixth chapter of Hebrews. A
man will fall into "a fury of fire" (Heb 10:27) who has
"spurned the Son of God, and profaned the blood of
the covenant by which he was sanctified, and outraged
the Spirit of grace" (Heb 10:29). Notice how the person
in question has already been "sanctified" by the "blood
of the covenant." This person has received the gift of
redemption of the New Covenant through the precious
blood of Christ. Yet, such a man will forfeit all those
benefits and fall into the fires of hell. Clearly, the epistle
to the Hebrews and the epistles of Paul in general teach
that the Christian can "fall from grace." This fall occurs
through apostasy or through committing mortal sin and
this accords perfectly with the Catholic doctrine of
salvation as it regards the possibility of falling from
grace.

Confession as the Ministry of Reconciliation

What happens if a baptized Christian commits a mortal
sin? According to Saint Paul, such a person "cannot
inherit the kingdom of God" (Gal 5:21). Mortal sin is a
rejection of the love of God, and as such, it deprives the
soul of grace. For this reason, Christ lovingly instituted
the sacrament of confession. The Catholic Church looks
to the evening of the day of Christ's resurrection as the
occasion on which Christ instituted this sacrament:

> Jesus came and stood among them and said to
> them, "Peace be with you." When He had said
> this, he showed them His hands and his side.
> Then the disciples were glad when they saw the
> Lord. Jesus said to them again, "Peace be with

you. As the Father has sent me, even so I send you." And when He had said this, He breathed on them, and said to them, *"Receive the Holy Spirit. If you forgive the sins of any, they are forgiven; if you retain the sins of any, they are retained"* (Jn 20:19-23)

It must be stated at the outset that the Catholic Church officially teaches that only God can forgive sins.[61] Returning to Saint Paul's doctrine of participation, the priests of the Catholic Church are given a share in Christ's power to forgive sins. Christ told the Apostles, "As the Father has sent me, even so I send you."

Saint Paul practiced the priestly power of binding and loosing sins during his apostolic ministry as we see in his words to the Corinthians:

> For though absent in body I am present in spirit, and as if present, I have already pronounced judgment in the name of the Lord Jesus on the man who has done such a thing. When you are assembled, and my spirit is present, with the power of our Lord Jesus, you are to deliver this man to Satan for the destruction of the flesh, that his spirit may be saved in the day of the Lord Jesus (1 Cor 5:3-6).

Paul, through his participation in the high priesthood of Christ, is able to "pronounce judgment" against a sinner. In his Second Epistle to the Corinthians, Paul explains his unique ministry of reconciliation that he and Timothy exercise. Notice how Paul speaks of "us" as referring to Paul and Timothy and of "you" as to the lay people of Corinth:

> All this is from God, who through Christ
> reconciled us to himself and gave to us the
> ministry of reconciliation; that is, in Christ God
> was reconciling the world to himself, not
> counting their trespasses against them, and
> entrusting to us the message of reconciliation.
> So we are ambassadors for Christ, God making
> his appeal through us. We beseech you on
> behalf of Christ, be reconciled to God. For our
> sake he made him to be sin who knew no sin, so
> that in him we might become the righteousness
> of God (2 Cor 5:18-21).

For this reason, the Catholic Church calls confession
the "sacrament of reconciliation." The sacrament of
reconciliation, or confession, involves contrition for sin,
confession of sin, and penance. The English word
"penance" comes from the Latin word *pænitentia*,
meaning "feeling regret" or "repentance." A penance is
a penitential act that outwardly demonstrates our
personal remorse. The Apostle Paul promoted these
penitential acts:

> I declared first to those at Damascus, then at
> Jerusalem and throughout all the country of
> Judea, and also to the Gentiles, that they should
> repent and turn to God and perform deeds
> worthy of their repentance (Acts 26:20).

Here Paul explains that he preaches not only that people
should repent, but also that they should "perform deeds
worthy of their repentance." This is the very definition
of the word "penance." However, all Christians should
be careful that their performance of "deeds worthy of
their repentance" actually corresponds to an inward
conversion of heart. Otherwise, such penances become

sterile and false. However, true penance confirms us in
grace and allows us to become co-heirs with the risen
Christ, "provided we suffer with him" (Rom 8:17).

In agreement with Saint Paul, there is nothing
that we can do to save ourselves. We do not believe that
the penances that we perform actually merit our
salvation. The Church seeks to guard against this error:

> This degree of satisfaction appease sGod and
> renders Him propitious to us; and it is a
> satisfaction for which we are indebted to Christ
> our Lord alone, who paid the price of our sins
> on the cross, and offered to God a
> superabundant satisfaction. No created being
> could have been of such worth as to deliver us
> from so heavy a debt.[62]

We learn from Paul's Second Epistle to the Corinthians
that the man who had been excommunicated by Paul
was again reconciled to the Church (2 Cor 2:6-8). We
also learn that this man underwent some sort of
penance imposed by the Church, and so we see that the
Catholic priest's ministry of binding and loosing
hearkens back to the priestly ministry of Saint Paul.

NOTES

[57] Saint Augustine, *Treatise on Rebuke and Grace*, 9
(VI). Philip Schaff, *The Nicene and Post-Nicene Fathers* Vol.
5, 475.

[58] May God grant that I might one day complete
a book on Augustine similar to this one on Paul—*The
Catholic Faith of Augustine*—a volume refuting the
Protestant claim that Augustine belongs to the so-called
Reformation.

NOTES CONTINUED

[59] *Catechism of Trent,* 264.

[60] *Reconciliatio et paenitentia,* 17 §12.

[61] *Catechism of Trent,* 242.

[62] *Catechism of Trent,* 272.

6. PAUL ON PURGATORY
& PRAYER FOR THE DEAD

...he will be saved, but only as through fire...
1 CORINTHIANS 3:15

Post-Mortem Purgation

NO DOUBT, THIS CHAPTER should raise some eyebrows among the Protestants reading this book. Many non-Catholic students of Paul's writings assume that purgatory is the farthest thing from the mind of Paul. However, the Catholic Church finds one of the most persuasive arguments for purgatory within Paul's letters. This difference is accounted for by the fact that most Protestants have learned that purgatory is a halfway house between heaven and hell. This presupposition is incorrect. Purgatory is not the middle ground between heaven and hell. Rather, purgatory is a preparation and purification for heaven:

> a special place of purification, the Union Councils of Lyons and of Florence uphold the purifying fire and the expiatory character of the penal sufferings: The souls of those who depart this life with true repentance and the love of God, before they have rendered satisfaction for their trespasses and negligences by the worthy fruits of penance, are

purified   after   death   the   punishments   of purifications."[63]

We learn from Christ that "everyone will be salted with fire" (Mk 9:49) and that there is the possibility of forgiveness "in the age to come" (Mt 12:32). Saint Gregory the Great (pope from A.D. 590 to 604), commenting on this last passage, observed:

> As for certain lesser faults, we must believe that, before the Final Judgment, there is a purifying fire. He who is truth says that whoever utters blasphemy against the Holy Spirit will be pardoned neither in this age nor in the age to come. From this sentence we understand that certain offenses can be forgiven in this age, but certain others in the age to come.[64]

Christ also speaks of a situation where Christians may be locked up and "will not get out till you have paid the last penny" (Mt 5:26). Here, Christians should ask themselves, "What does Christ mean when He says that we might be locked up *until we pay*"? Locked up where? Paying for what?

In this passage, Christ speaks of us having to pay our debts on account of lacking charity. Clearly, Christ is not speaking of hell since he says, "you will not get out *till* you have paid the last penny." Because hell is eternal, no one ever "gets out" of it. Also, Christ cannot mean that we need to pay copper pennies to God. Since this passage belongs to the Sermon on the Mount, it is also not the case that Christ is giving us practical advice about settling debts with one's neighbor in order to avoid jail time. Instead, Christ is warning us about spiritual debts that will be paid in a place where we can eventually "get out."

Christ here describes the punishment that Christians will receive for not forgiving their neighbors as they wish to be forgiven. This "debt of sin" is paid in purgatory. Yet these passages do not stand alone. This is a book on Paul, so we must highlight the fact that the Catholic Church looks to Saint Paul as one of the chief witnesses to the existence of purgatory.

Protestants sometimes object to the doctrine of purgatory by citing Paul's statement, "And I am sure that he who began a good work in you will bring it to completion at the day of Jesus Christ" (Phil 1:6). However, if we look closely at this verse, we discover that it is actually an argument in favor of purgatory. The good work initiated in us by God is not necessarily completed on the day of our death. Rather, Saint Paul indicates that the completion of the good work continues after death and even until the judgment day of Jesus Christ. This statement by Paul, far from condemning purgatory, actually confirms the Catholic teaching that God continues to make us righteous even after death.

Many Evangelicals also wrongly attribute to Paul this saying: "To be absent from the body is to be present with the Lord." However, if we examine the passage, we discover that Saint Paul actually wrote, "we would *rather* be absent from the body and at home with the Lord" (2 Cor 5:8). Paul is stating a preference, not a matter of fact. Only two verses later, Paul states that even Christians must "appear before the judgment seat of Christ, so that each one may receive good or evil, according to what he has done in the body" (2 Cor 5:10). Elsewhere, in his First Epistle to the Corinthians, Paul explains how each man's life will be tested with fire after he dies:

> For no other foundation can any one lay than that which is laid, which is Jesus Christ. Now if any one builds on the foundation with gold, silver, precious stones, wood, hay, straw—each man's work will become manifest. For the Day will disclose it, because it will be revealed with fire, and the fire will

> test what sort of work each one has done. If the
> work that any man has built on the foundation
> survives, he will receive a reward. If any man's
> work is burned up, he will suffer loss, though he
> himself will be saved, but only as through fire (1
> Cor 3:11-15).

Saint Augustine interprets this passage in Saint Paul as
pertaining to the purgatorial fires after death saying, "some
believers shall pass through a kind of purgatorial fire."[65] In
the passage above, Saint Paul explains that Christians may
pass through fire after their deaths. If they have lived well,
they "will receive a reward"; if not, then they "will suffer
loss" without being damned to the fires of hell. This
purgatorial fire cleanses them for heaven, as Paul states:
"he himself will be saved, but only as through fire." We
should remember that Saint Paul originally wrote in Greek,
and the Greek word used by Saint Paul for the saving fire
of the afterlife is *puros*. The Catholic Church uses the word
puros as the root for its word describing this state of
cleansing fire: *pur*-gatory.[66] The purifying fires after death
cleanse the soul and make it ready to meet the Lord in the
radiance of sanctity. Saint Augustine further elaborated on
this Paul's description of the believer's final purgation:

> That there should be some fire even after this life is
> not incredible, and it can be inquired into and
> either be discovered or left hidden whether some of
> the faithful may be saved, some more slowly and
> some more quickly in the greater or lesser degree in
> which they loved the good things that perish,
> *through a certain purgatorial fire.*[67]

This purgatorial fire is deemed necessary because "without
holiness, no one will see the Lord" (Heb 12:14). If we die
before we are perfectly sanctified, then the Holy Spirit

mercifully continues the process. We also learn that heaven contains the "the spirits of just men who have been "made righteous" (Heb 12:23). The Greek phrase that Saint Paul uses is *diakaion teteleiomenon.*[68] The verb *teteleiomenon* is a perfect passive participle denoting a now completed event that occurred over time. In other words, "having been made righteous," from a grammatical point of view, is a progressive event—not an instantaneous one. This implies that the dead were made righteous and holy. For this reason, C.S. Lewis made a remarkable case for purgatory based on this Pauline teaching that the soul destined for heaven must first be cleansed by purgatorial fire. Lewis held that the Christian should desire the fires of purgatory since he would wish to enter into the courts of the Lord fully bathed, wearing clean clothes, and even with fresh breath:

> Our souls demand Purgatory, don't they? Would it not break the heart if God said to us, 'It is true, my son, that your breath smells and your rags drip with mud and slime, but we are charitable here and no one will upbraid you with these things, nor draw away from you. Enter into the joy'? Should we not reply, 'With submission, sir, and if there is no objection, I'd rather be cleaned first.' 'It may hurt, you know' 'Even so, sir.'

> I assume that the process of purification will normally involve suffering. Partly from tradition; partly because most real good that has been done me in this life has involved it. But I don't think the suffering is the purpose of the purgation. I can well believe that people neither much worse nor much better than I will suffer less than I or more…The treatment given will be the one required, whether it hurts little or much.

> My favorite image on this matter comes from the dentist's chair. I hope that when the tooth of life is drawn and I am 'coming round', a voice will say, 'Rinse your mouth out with this.' This will be Purgatory. The rinsing may take longer than I can now imagine. The taste of this may be more fiery and astringent than my present sensibility could endure.[69]

It should come as no surprise to us that our Heavenly Father would lovingly purify us through suffering. Every good parent allows his child to suffer when it leads to the child's greater good. We shall examine Paul's doctrine of redemptive suffering in a later chapter. Here let it suffice to say that God is our Father and we are His children. Because of this, we should expect to be disciplined in this life, and if necessary, in the life to come until we are ready to gaze upon the Lord face to face. The epistle to the Hebrews explains how Christians should expect to be disciplined by their heavenly Father:

> For the Lord disciplines him whom he loves, and chastises every son whom he receives. It is for discipline that you have to endure. God is treating you as sons; for what son is there whom his father does not discipline? If you are left without discipline, in which all have participated, then you are illegitimate children and not sons.
>
> For the moment all discipline seems painful rather than pleasant; later it yields the peaceful fruit of righteousness to those who have been trained by it (Heb 12:6-11).

Consequently, we discover that there is a difference between suffering the wrath of God (hell) and experiencing the loving discipline of God (in this life and in purgatory). This difference that we find between eternal wrath and temporary discipline is the basis for the Catholic Church's important distinction between eternal punishment and temporal punishment.

Protestants commonly cite the passage about the dying thief on the cross in Mark 23:43 as evidence that purgatory does not exist: "I tell you the truth, today you will be with me in Paradise." However, this objection fails to understand that initial justification and regeneration (as in baptism) remits both eternal punishment and temporal punishment. For the rest of us, who are converted earlier in life and then fail to cooperate with the grace of conversion, we thereby gain temporal punishment and the need for purgatory. Hence, the dying thief did not require purgatory, because his conversion or *baptismus flaminis* occurred just before his death, so he was already cleansed and had no chance to sin afterward. However, those of us who live long lives as Christians beyond our initial conversions and who also fail to sanctify our lives may require purgatory, because we have squandered the grace we received. Likewise, a deceased baptized child would not go to purgatory, but a sixty-year-old Catholic man likely would go to purgatory if he lived a life of grace but did not earnestly pursue sanctification. This complicated matter of eternal punishment and temporal punishment deserves special treatment.

Eternal Punishment and Temporal Punishment

The Catholic Church teaches that sin has a double consequence. Mortal sin, as discussed above, deprives us of our fellowship with God. The consequence of this is "eternal punishment." Eternal punishment is the eternal sufferings of hell. Saint Paul describes this eternal punishment as "the punishment of eternal destruction and

exclusion from the presence of the Lord" (2 Thess 1:9). As
Paul explains elsewhere, "the wages of sin is death" (Rom
3:23). When a believer is justified by faith for the first time
in baptism, or at subsequent times through the sacrament
of reconciliation, the *eternal* punishment of hell is expiated
through the passion, death, and resurrection of Christ.
However, *temporal* punishments remain. This is especially
true on the natural level. For example, if you murder
someone, you may repent and receive forgiveness through
Christ. Nevertheless, Christ's forgiveness does not mean
that you won't be punished in prison. If you commit
adultery, you may repent and receive forgiveness through
Christ. However, you may contract a venereal disease or
have a child out of wedlock. The forgiveness that we
receive from Christ doesn't magically reverse all the
negative effects of sin in the world.

The classic example of temporal punishment is
found in the life of King David. He committed adultery
with Bathsheba and arranged for her husband to be killed.
When the prophet Nathan confronted David, the king
repented.

> David said to Nathan, "I have sinned against the
> Lord." And Nathan said to David, "The Lord also
> has put away your sin. You shall not die.
> Nevertheless, because by this deed you have utterly
> scorned the LORD, the child that is born to you
> shall die" (2 Sam 12:13-14).

David escaped the eternal punishment of God, but he still
had to face certain temporal punishments on account of his
sin.

Another example of temporal punishment derives
from the story of Adam and Eve. Adam and Eve sinned
against God but received forgiveness and the promise of a
Savior (Gen 3:15). Nevertheless, they received temporal

punishments. God gave to Eve and to all subsequent women the temporal punishment of pain in childbearing (Gen 3:16), and God gave to Adam and to all subsequent men the temporal punishment of toilsome labor for the sustenance of life (Gen 3:17).

Whenever we sin, we introduce into the world a certain imbalance. Our sins offend God and hurt others. Our sins even hurt ourselves. Although we can never make full reparation for the sins that we have committed, we should seek to make amends by making a heartfelt apology or recompense for what we have done. We take on punishments that we deserve. If a Christian wishes to cheat the system through seeking to escape eternal punishment, but avoiding the consequences of sin, then he will find himself passing through the fires of purgatory with his head hung low. As Saint Paul explained, "he himself will be saved, but only as through fire" (1 Cor 3:15). The Catholic Church does, however, teach that one can avoid purgatory altogether. ""If the baptized person fulfills the obligations demanded of a Christian, he does well. If he does not–provided he keeps the faith, without which he would perish forever–no matter in what sin or impurity remains, he will be saved, as it were, by fire; as one who has built on the foundation, which is Christ, not gold, silver, and precious stones, but wood, hay straw, that is, not just and chasted works but wicked and unchaste works."[70]

In summary, temporal punishment is what we experience in purgatory, which is entirely different from the eternal punishment of the damned. The distinction between the eternal punishment of hell and the temporal punishment of purgatory was officially proclaimed in 1336 by Pope Benedict XII in his constitution *Benedictus Deus*. Most misunderstandings about purgatory result from failing to make the distinction between eternal punishment and temporal punishment. Nevertheless, Saint Paul firmly exhorts the Christians of his day to joyfully enter into this kind of temporal punishment so that they may be ushered into God's presence without hindrance. "We are children of God, and if children, then heirs, heirs of God and fellow heirs with Christ, provided we suffer with him in order that we may also be glorified with him" (Rom 8:16-17).

Praying for the Dead

Since Paul was once a Pharisee, we know that he prayed for the dead. The Pharisees and all orthodox Jews of our day pray for the repose of the souls of the departed. This practice goes hand in hand with belief in the resurrection of the dead. We also know that the Apostle Paul prayed for the dead because he accepted as canonical the book of Second Maccabees, which itself endorses the practice of praying for the dead.

Here we must follow a tangent and examine the status of seven Old Testament books that were rejected from the canon of Scripture by Martin Luther, the so-called *apocrypha*, or "hidden" books. These include the following seven books:

Tobit
Judith
Wisdom
Sirach or Ecclesiasticus
Baruch
1 Maccabees
2 Maccabees

The Council of Rome first officially proclaimed the canon of the Bible in A.D. 382, and the list of Scriptural books included these seven deuterocanonical books. These books had been rejected by the Pharisees at the end of the first century because of their emphasis on the Messiah and the resurrection. For example, the description of the condemned Messiah in the second chapter of the book of Wisdom is one of the Old Testament's most vivid prophecies of Christ's passion and death under Pontius Pilate. Even though the rabbis came to reject these seven books, the Church continued to cite them as Scripture. They were included in the Septuagint, the accepted Greek translation of the Old Testament. We observe in the writings of Paul that he almost always cites the Old Testament from this Septuagint version. Paul also repeatedly cites and refers to the deuterocanonical book of Wisdom. This fact alone tells us that the Bible employed by Paul was the Septuagint—the Bible version that included these seven deuterocanonical books. Paul also refers to back 2 Maccabees 13:4 in 1 Timothy 6:15 (God as "King of Kings"). His epistle to the Hebrews 11:35 also refers to an episode that is described in detail in 2 Maccabees 7:1-42. This further demonstrates that Paul counted the deuterocanonical books, and particularly Second Maccabees, as belonging to Sacred Scripture.

It is important that we establish this fact because the strongest case for praying for the dead is found in the book of Second Maccabees where Judah Maccabaeus takes up a collection for sacrifice to be offered for his dead soldiers and instructs that prayer be made for them.

> He also took up a collection, man by man, to the amount of two thousand drachmas of silver, and sent it to Jerusalem to provide for a sin offering. In doing this he acted very well and honorably, taking account of the resurrection. For if he were not expecting that those who had fallen would rise again, it would have been superfluous and foolish to pray for the dead (2 Macc 12:43-44).

This episode happened in Judea about one hundred and sixty years before the birth of Christ. This proves that the

Jews before Christ not only prayed for the dead but that the priests at the Temple in Jerusalem made sacrifices on behalf of those who had died. If Second Maccabees is part of Sacred Scripture, then it goes without saying that praying for the dead is commendable and proper. And if we pray for the dead, then there must be some state in the afterlife that is neither hell nor heaven. In other words, we have a primitive notion of purgatory.

We also have two examples from the writings of Saint Paul that indicate that prayer was made for those Christians who had died. The most vivid comes from the Second Epistle to Timothy:

> May the Lord grant mercy to the household of Onesiphorus, for he often refreshed me; he was not ashamed of my chains, but when he arrived in Rome he searched for me eagerly and found me. May the Lord grant him to find mercy from the Lord on that Day—and you well know all the service he rendered at Ephesus (2 Tim 1:16-18).

Saint Paul speaks of Onesiphorus in a way that indicates that he is now dead. He asks that "the Lord grant mercy to the household of Onesiphorus," since the family is certainly grieving. Paul then eulogizes Onesiphorus for his heroic Christian service. Finally, Saint Paul prays for Onesiphorus: "May the Lord grant him to find mercy from the Lord on that Day." Later in the same epistle, Paul again uses the phrase "that Day," referring to the final judgment day of Christ (2 Tim 4:8). In Paul's final salutation, he again salutes "the household of Onesiphorus" (2 Tim 4:19) without mention of Onesiphorus himself. If Onesiphorus had been alive, we would expect that Paul would greet him. All indications lead to the conclusion that Onesiphorus is dead and awaiting the judgment of "that Day."

The second passage is a difficult one. It is the passage in which Paul mentions the baptisms for the dead:

> Otherwise, what do people mean by being baptized on behalf of the dead? If the dead are not raised at all, why are people baptized on their behalf? (1 Cor 15:29)

One can observe a similarity in Paul's statement and the one made in Second Maccabees:

> For if he were not expecting that those who had fallen would rise again, it would have been superfluous and foolish to pray for the dead (2 Macc 12:44).

Tradition proposes that the Corinthian novelty of baptizing for the dead was a superstitious act and not in conformity with the apostolic custom.[71] Paul mentions it not by way of approval but for polemical purposes. In other words, Paul mentions baptisms for the dead not to approve the custom but to rebuke the Corinthians by citing how they contradicted themselves in contrary errors. How could the Corinthian Christians deny the resurrection of Christ and then baptize living people in the place of dead people in hope that the dead would be resurrected? The presupposition underneath the practice is that the faithful on earth can assist those who have died in some way. Right or wrong in their intentions, the Christians in Corinth were following the Jewish instinct described in Second Maccabees. They believed that those still living on earth could assist those who had departed through death.

Hence, we come to see that the Catholic Church's doctrine of purgatory finds ancient expression in the works of Saint Paul for four reasons. First, the Apostle speaks of post-mortem salvation "through fire" (1 Cor 3:15). The

Greek word *puros* corresponds to *pur*-gation. Second, we also see that Paul accepted the canonical text of Second Maccabees, an Old Testament book that commends prayers and sacrifice for the dead. Third, we have an example of Paul praying for the dead when he commends his departed friend Onesiphorus to the mercy of God in preparation for "that Day" (2 Tim 1:18). Lastly, we have the unusual words of the Apostle regarding baptisms for the dead, which in the very least demonstrate that prayer for the dead was something assumed by the earliest Christians. From these Pauline texts we can see how the early Church prayed for the dead to be delivered from purgatorial fire from the very beginning—because it was the Jewish practice to do so.[72]

In the second century, Tertullian explains, "We make sacrifices for the dead on the anniversary day of their birthday." Likewise, Saint Augustine described his dying mother's request to have her named commemorated at the Holy Sacrifice of the Mass for her delivery from purgatory. About his mother Saint Monica, he writes:

> These things she entrusted not to us, but only desired to have her name remembered at Thy altar, which she had served without the omission of a single day. Whence she knew that the holy sacrifice was dispensed, by which the handwriting that was against us is blotted out; by which the enemy was triumphed over, who, summing up our offences, and searching for something to bring against us, found nothing in Him in whom we conquer.[73]

Likewise, the great Saint John Chrysostom (347-407) commended prayers for the dead:

> Let us help and commemorate them. If Job's sons were purified by their father's sacrifice, why would

we doubt that our offerings for the dead bring them some consolation? Let us not hesitate to help those who have died and to offer our prayers for them.[74]

The references in Saint Augustine and Saint Chrysostom regarding offering of sacrifice for the dead naturally lead us to the question regarding the nature of sacrifice in the New Testament. How do Christians offer sacrifice to God if Christ's death on the cross was the once-for-all sacrifice to the Father? The Catholic Church has always held that the Eucharist is the same sacrifice of Christ on Calvary. To better understand this mystery, let us now turn Saint Paul's doctrine of the Holy Eucharist, especially as it regards Eucharistic sacrifice.

NOTES

[63] Ludwig Ott, *Fundamentals of Catholic Dogma*, 483.

[64] Saint Gregory the Great, *Dialogues* 4, 39; (*Patrologia Latina* 77, 396).

[65] Saint Augustine, *Enchiridion* 68-69. For more on Augustine's doctrine of Purgatory, see also *City of God* 21, 26.

[66] The Greek word *puros,* meaning "fire," is etymologically related to the Latin word *purus,* meaning "clean, clear, unmixed," since fire cleanses and sterilizes. Fire is also used in metallurgy to separate impurities. Each word derives from the Proto-Indo-European base *peu-/pu-,* meaning "to purify, cleanse" (the same root is also related to the Sanskrit word *pavate* meaning "purify, cleanse").

NOTES CONTINUED

[67] Saint Augustine, *Enchiridion* 18, 69.

[68] δικαίων τετελειωμένων.

[69] C.S. Lewis, *Letters To Malcolm: Chiefly on Prayer*, 108-109.

[70] Saint Augustine, *Faith and Works* 1:1 (A.D. 413).

[71] Tertullian offers another suggestion by stating Saint Paul referred to the baptism of the body, which he called "the body of death" in Rom 7:24. See Tertullian, *Against Marcion* 5, 10.

[72] Taylor Marshall, *The Crucified Rabbi—Judaism and the Origins of Catholic Christianity* (Dallas: Saint John Press, 2009).

[73] Saint Augustine, *Confessions* 9, 13.

[74] Saint John Chrysostom, *Homilies on First Corinthians,* 41, 5.(*Patrologia Graeca* 61, 361); cf. Job 1:5.

7. PAUL ON THE EUCHARISTIC SACRIFICE

> …the bread which we break
> is a participation in the Body of Christ…
> 1 CORINTHIANS 10:16

WE BEGAN THIS BOOK by proposing that the concept of participation is central to the Apostle Paul's theology. Christians, according to Saint Paul, have become partakers of the life, death, and resurrection of Christ. As Paul wrote to the Corinthians, "But he who is united to the Lord becomes one spirit with Him" (1 Cor 6:17). And again, "For if we have been united with him in a death like his, we shall certainly be united with him in a resurrection like his" (Rom 6:5).

Perhaps one of the most profound passages demonstrating how Paul viewed himself as a partaker of Christ is his statement in Galatians:

> With Christ I am nailed to the cross. And I live, now not I, but Christ lives in me. And that I live now in the flesh, I live in the faith of the Son of God, who loved me and delivered himself for me (Gal 2:19–20).

Paul believes that the life of the believer is taken up into the life of Christ. This theological insight, as discussed in the first chapter, derives from Paul's conversion to Christ where Christ asked him, "Why do you persecute *me?*" Paul's persecution of Christians was indeed a persecution of Christ because those Christians participated in the life of Christ. We find the same idea in the high priestly prayer of our Lord Jesus Christ:

> The glory which thou hast given me I have given to them, that they may be one even as we are one, *I in them and thou in me*, that they may become perfectly one, so that the world may know that thou hast sent me and hast loved them even as thou hast loved me...I made known to them thy name, and I will make it known, that the love with which thou hast loved me may be in them, *and I in them* (Jn 17:22-23, 26).

What Does Eucharist Mean?

Paul's doctrine of the believer's participation in Christ finds its high point in the Apostle's doctrine of the Eucharist, which he called "the Supper of the Lord" (1 Cor 11:20) or "the Breaking of the Bread" (Acts 20:7). Some time before A.D. 100, the ritual of the Lord's Supper came to be known as the *Eucharist*. We find the term *Eucharist* being applied to the Lord's Supper in the *Didache*, a first-century document: "Now as regards the Eucharist, give thanks after this manner."[75]

There are two reasons for why the Lord's Supper came to be known as the Eucharist. The first is that the Greek word *eucharistia* means "giving thanks." The earliest use of *eucharistia* in the context of the Lord's Supper is found in First Corinthians where Saint Paul used a Greek form of the word *eucharistia* to describe how the Lord's Supper was celebrated:

> And when he had given thanks [Greek: *eucharistésas* or "eucharisted"], he broke it, and

said, "This is my body which is for you. Do this in remembrance of me" (1 Cor 11:24).

Saint Paul's First Epistle to the Corinthians was written in about A.D. 57. Some regard this epistle to be the earliest written testimony to the ritual and beliefs surrounding the Supper of the Lord. Less than one hundred years after the death of Saint Paul, we find Saint Justin Martyr writing to the pagan Emperor Antonius Pius (A.D. 138-161) in order to explain the way in which Christians at this time celebrated the Eucharist:

> On the day we call the "Day of the Sun" {i.e. Sunday}, all who dwell in the city or country gather in the same place.

> The memoirs of the Apostles and the writings of the Prophets are read, as much as time permits. When the reader has finished, he who presides over those gathered admonishes and challenges them to imitate these beautiful things.

> Then we all rise together and offer prayers for ourselves and for all others, wherever they may be, so that we may be found righteous by our life and actions, and faithful to the commandments so as to obtain eternal salvation. When the prayers are concluded we exchange the kiss.

> Then someone brings bread and a cup of water and wine mixed together to him who presides over the brethren. He takes them and offers praise and glory to the Father of the universe, through the name of the Son and of the Holy Spirit and for a considerable time he gives

> thanks ["he eucharists"] that we have been judged worthy of these gifts. When he has concluded the prayers and thanksgivings, all present give voice to an acclamation by saying: "Amen!"
>
> When he who presides has given thanks and the people have responded, those whom we call deacons give to those present the *eucharisted* bread, wine and water and take them to those who are absent.[76]

Here we find not only the use of Paul's word *eucharistia*, but also the structure that the Apostle laid down in the Church at Corinth. Let us now turn to those passages in the tenth and eleventh chapters of First Corinthians in which Saint Paul explains the meaning of the Eucharist.

Eucharistic Sacrifice

The second reason why the Lord's Supper came to be known as the Eucharist is that the Greek word *eucharistia,* meaning "thanksgiving," corresponded perfectly to the Old Testament sacrifice known as the *todah* offering. In Hebrew, the word *todah* also means "thanksgiving." Accordingly, the New Testament authors use the word *eucharistia* as a Greek translation of the Hebrew *todah,* meaning "thanksgiving sacrifice." In the Old Testament, we read that the *todah* thanksgiving sacrifices were offered with wheat flour and wine (Num 15:1-10). This sacrifice of wheat and wine evokes the sacrifice of bread and wine offered by Melchizedek, who blessed the patriarch Abraham (Gen 14:18). Moreover, we learn that Christ is a "priest according to the order of Melchizedek" (Heb 7:1-17); Jews would therefore expect the Messiah to offer a sacrifice of bread and wine. Moreover, we read that King David offered the *todah* sacrifice with bread and wine (1 Chr 16:3). We also read about how the prophet Jonah, having been swallowed by the whale, vowed to the Lord a *todah* sacrifice if he should be delivered from death after spending three days in darkness (Jon 2:3-10).

The earliest Christians came to perceive that the Last Supper of Christ was in fact a *todah* sacrifice of bread and wine in union with the sacrifice of Christ. The Davidic *todah* thanksgiving sacrifice and the promised *todah* thanksgiving sacrifice of Jonah, who also rose from the belly of the fish on the third day, confirmed that the wheat and wine ritual of Christ hearkened back to the bread and wine "thanksgiving" sacrifice of the Old Testament.[77]

Consequently, the Catholic Church teaches that the Eucharist is not merely a meal but the one true sacrifice of Christ, re-presented throughout the ages. Martin Luther and subsequent Protestants rejected the sacrificial aspect of the Eucharist. Citing Hebrews 10:10, Protestants held that Christ died "once for all." They could not perceive how every single Eucharistic celebration of the Holy Sacrifice of the Mass could also be that same sacrifice of Christ offered "once for all" on the cross. It seemed to them that the Catholic Church taught that Christ was repeatedly slain and sacrificed over and over upon every altar of the Catholic Church. If this were true, it would have been a grave error indeed. However, the Catholic Church, in agreement with the epistle to the Hebrews, does not teach that Christ dies repeatedly on the altar. Rather, the Church agrees that Christ died "once for all"—*once for all time*. Christ died once, but the application of this sacrifice is for *all time* and for *all people*. Christ does not die again, but the single offering of His body and blood on the cross is re-presented in the Eucharistic sacrifice of the Mass and applied to those who receive Holy

Communion. In other words, the sacrifice on Calvary and the sacrifice on the altar are one and the same, their mode being different. The Catholic Council of Trent (1545-1563) in the wake of the Protestant Reformation explained the mystery of Christ's one sacrifice and the sacrifice of the Eucharist in detail:

> He, therefore, our God and Lord, though He was about to offer Himself once on the altar of the cross unto God the Father, by means of his death, there to operate an eternal redemption; nevertheless, because that His priesthood was not to be extinguished by His death, in the last supper, on the night in which He was betrayed—that He might leave, to His own beloved Spouse the Church, a visible sacrifice, such as the nature of man requires, whereby that bloody sacrifice, *once to be accomplished on the cross, might be represented, and the memory thereof remain even unto the end of the world*, and its salutary virtue be applied to the remission of those sins which we daily commit.[78]

The Council of Trent then cites the Apostle Paul as evidence for the doctrine of Eucharistic sacrifice:

> The Apostle Paul, writing to the Corinthians, has not obscurely indicated, when he says, that they who are defiled by the participation of the table of devils, cannot be partakers of the table of the Lord; by the table, meaning in both places the altar.[79]

The Council of Trent is, of course, referring to the passage in First Corinthians where Paul compares the

sacrifice of the Christian Eucharist to the sacrifices of
Israel and the sacrifices of pagans:

> The chalice of blessing which we bless, is it not
> a participation in the blood of Christ? The bread
> which we break, is it not a participation in the
> Body of Christ? Because there is one bread, we
> who are many are one Body, for we all partake
> of the one bread.
>
> Consider the people of Israel. Are not those
> who eat the sacrifices partners in the altar? What
> do I imply then? That food offered to idols is
> anything, or that an idol is anything? No, I imply
> that what pagans sacrifice they offer to demons
> and not to God. I do not want you to be
> partners with demons. You cannot drink the
> chalice of the Lord and the chalice of demons.
> You cannot partake of the table of the Lord and
> the table of demons (1 Cor 10:18-21).

Here again we find a striking example of Paul's doctrine
of participation. First, Christians participate in the body
and blood of Jesus Christ through the Eucharist.
Second, the people of Israel who ate the Old Testament
sacrifices were "partners in the altar." Third, pagans
who sacrifice meat to idols, that is to say demons,
become "partners with demons." Last of all, Paul
concludes that a Christian "cannot partake of the table
of the Lord and the table of demons." Just as Israelite
sacrifices and pagan sacrifices allowed worshippers to
partake of spiritual realities through their altars, so also
Christians become partakers of the sacrifice of Christ
through the Eucharist.

A plain reading of First Corinthians reveals that
the Apostle Paul identifies the "Lord's table" as an

"altar." The Protestant rejection of a sacrificial altar is especially unwarranted when we consider that the epistle to the Hebrews explicitly states that the Church of Jesus Christ worships at an altar from which we eat and drink the sacrifice of Christ:

> *We have an altar* from which those who serve the tent [i.e. the Old Testament tabernacle] have no right to *eat.* For the *bodies* of those animals whose *blood* is brought into the sanctuary by the high priest *as a sacrifice* for sin are burned outside the camp. *So Jesus also suffered* outside the gate in order to sanctify the people *through his own blood* (Heb 13:10-13, *emphases* mine).

The passage above indicates that Christians possess an altar that corresponds to the altar of the Jewish tabernacle in Jerusalem. Whereas the Jewish people sacrificed the body and blood of bulls and goats on that altar, Christians have an altar from which even the Jewish priests "have no right to eat." The sacrifice which the Christians eat is "Jesus who suffered" and who sanctified "the people through his own blood." The passage no doubt refers to the Christian Eucharist of which Christians have a right to eat as partakers of Christ. If we peel back the English translation of Hebrews 13:10-13, we see that the Greek word for altar is *thusiasterion*. This word is a compound of the Greek word *thusia* {"sacrifice"} and *sterion* {"fixed place"}. To render it literally, Hebrews 13:10 reads: "We have a *fixed place of sacrifice.*" The concept of Eucharistic sacrifice is built in to the very word for altar as a Christian place of sacrifice.

The Real Presence of Christ in the Eucharist

If Saint Paul's view of Christianity is that of participation in the life of Christ, then we would expect that there must be a way for this participation to be realized in the daily life of the Christian. For this reason, the heart of Paul's doctrine of participation is the Real Presence of Christ in the Eucharist.

In First Corinthians, Paul speaks of the Eucharist in the highest regard because "the chalice of blessing is a participation in the blood of Christ" and "the bread which we break is a participation in the Body of Christ" (1 Cor 10:16). The Greek word used by Paul for "participation" in this context is *koinonia*. The Latin Vulgate translated this Greek word both as *communicatio* and as *participatio*. Those who receive Holy Communion are thereby called "communicants." The old Douay-Rheims Bible translated it as *communion,* and so even today, English speakers refer to receiving the Holy Eucharist as receiving Holy Communion.[80]

The Apostle goes on to say that "Because there is one bread, we who are many are one body, for we all partake of the one bread" (1 Cor 10:17). The earliest Christians recognized that union with God in the Eucharist established union with the Church. Near the year 250, Saint Cyprian bishop of Carthage observed this Eucharistic mystery:

> In this very sacrament our people are shown to be made one, so that in like manner as many grains, collected, and ground, and mixed together into one mass, make one bread, so also in Christ, who is the heavenly bread, we may know that there is one body, with which our number is joined and united.[81]

According to Paul, the Eucharist not only brings us into communion with Christ but it also brings us into communion with one another. For this reason, the Holy Eucharist is the "source and summit of the Christian life."

Saint Paul continues his discussion of the Lord's Supper by rebuking the Corinthians for abusing the sacrament. It seems that the primitive expression of the Eucharist prior to A.D. 57 had still retained the feature of a meal. That is, the Eucharist, like the Last Supper of Christ, included a meal known as the *agape* or "love meal." This is evident in Christ's words of institution. He blessed and broke the bread. Then *when supper was ended*, Christ took the chalice and blessed it. It seems that a meal fell between these two events. Perhaps the inclusion of a meal was an early tradition or perhaps the Corinthians had wrongly imported a secular and social "pot-luck dinner" into what should have been a solemn occasion. Regardless, Saint Paul officially put an end to this arrangement and detached the fellowship meal from the actual rite of the Eucharist.[82] Paul rebukes them for their unbecoming behavior at the Eucharist, "For in eating, each one goes ahead with his own meal, and one is hungry and another is drunk. What! Do you not have houses to eat and drink in?" (1 Cor 11:21-22). In other words, "Eat your common meals at home. Don't bring food with you when you assemble for the Eucharist."

Saint Paul then reminds the Christians in Corinth of the essential formula for the Eucharist. Compare Paul's words to the current liturgy of the Roman Rite of the Catholic Church:[83]

1 Corinthians 11:23-26	*Catholic Consecration*
For I received from the Lord what I also delivered	Who the day before He was to suffer, He took

to you,

that the Lord Jesus on the night when he was betrayed took bread, and when he had given thanks, he broke it, saying:

bread in his holy and venerable hands, and with eyes raised to heaven to you, O God, his Almighty Father, giving you thanks He blessed it, broke the bread and gave it to his disciples, saying:

Take this, all of you, and eat it.

For this is my Body which is given up for you. Do this in remembrance of me.

For this is my Body which will be given up for you.

In a similar way, when supper was ended, he took the chalice saying:

In a similar way, when supper was ended, he took this precious chalice in his holy and venerable hands, and once more giving you thanks, He blessed it, and gave the chalice to his disciples, saying:

Take this, all of you, and drink from it.

For this chalice is the New Covenant in my Blood.

For this is the Chalice of my Blood, of the New and Everlasting Covenant, the mystery of faith, which for you and for many shall be poured out for the remission of sins.

As often as you drink it,	As often as you shall do
Do this in memory of me.	these things, you shall do
	them in memory of me.

This prayer is not a mere memorial. The Greek word used here for "memory" is *anamnesis,* which entails calling a past even into the present.[84] Moreover, every single time the word *anamnesis* occurs in the Bible, it appears in a sacrificial context.[85] When a duly ordained Catholic priest pronounces the words of consecration ("For this is my body" and "For this is the chalice of my blood") over the bread and the wine, the elements are converted into the body and blood of Christ. As the Council of Trent explained:

> By the consecration of the bread and of the wine, a conversion is made of the whole substance of the bread into the substance of the Body of Christ our Lord, and of the whole substance of the wine into the substance of His Blood; which conversion is, by the holy Catholic Church, suitably and properly called Transubstantiation.[86]

Transubstantiation denotes how God changes the substance of bread and wine into the substance of Christ, so that Christ is fully present in His sacred body, blood, soul, and divinity. We grant that Saint Paul did not use the term *transubstantiation.* One could hardly expect Paul, a Greek speaking Jew of the first century, to be acquainted with a Latin term. Similarly, Saint Paul did not use other Latinate words like *Trinity.* However, we can safely say that Paul taught the doctrine of the Trinity without using the Latin term *Trinitas.*[87] Similarly, the Catholic Church employs the term *transubstantiation* as the best description of the doctrine of the Real Presence of Christ in the Eucharist as proposed by Saint Paul in First Corinthians.

The conversion of the bread and wine into the body and blood of Christ is most evident when Paul explains the significance of the Eucharist: "Whoever, therefore, eats the bread or drinks the chalice of the Lord in an unworthy manner will be guilty of profaning the body and blood of the Lord" (1 Cor 11:27). Here the Apostle states the consequences attached to the Eucharist. Paul did not write, "Whoever, eats the bread or drinks the chalice of the Lord in an unworthy manner *will be guilty of a sin.*" He did not write, "Whoever, therefore, eats the bread or drinks the chalice of the Lord in an unworthy manner *will be guilty of mishandling holy things.*" Rather, Paul equated unworthy reception of the Holy Eucharist with the worst possible sin that a person could commit: the profanation of the body and blood of Christ. For Paul, the wrongful reception of the Holy Eucharist is tantamount to spitting on the crucified Christ or calling down a curse upon the body and blood of the Redeemer.

The language used by Paul cannot be reconciled with a symbolic interpretation. His language evokes episodes of the Old Testament in which men died instantly for irreverence toward the holy things of God, as in the case of Uzzah and the Ark of the Covenant (2 Sam 6:6-7). How much worse is it to profane the very Son of God! Moreover, Saint Paul explains that many Christians in Corinth were sick and even dead because they had approached the Holy Eucharist unworthily (1 Cor 11:30). Again, it is hard to see how a mere symbol could kill someone.

Since the consecrated elements become the body and blood of Christ, Paul warns the Christians in Corinth and the Christians of every age: "Let a man examine himself, and so eat of the bread and drink of the chalice" (1 Cor 11:28). In response to Saint Paul's exhortation, every celebration of the Holy Sacrifice of the Mass begins with a penitential rite that includes a general confession of sin and an invocation of the Lord's mercy. Moreover, any Catholic Christian who has committed a mortal sin is instructed not to receive the Holy Eucharist until he has received absolution through the sacrament of reconciliation.

Christ Our Passover

So far we have focused on the warning of Saint Paul against unworthily receiving the Eucharist. Let us now turn to the great benefits that can be received from the Eucharist. The Holy Eucharist is the daily bread by which Catholic Christians are spiritually nourished. This is why attending the Holy Sacrifice of the Mass is essential for the Catholic. The English word *Mass* derives from the Latin word *missa*. This is the same Latin word from which we derive the English words *dismissal* and *mission*. Among the last words recited by the priest or deacon in the Holy Sacrifice of the Mass are: *Ite missa est*. The phrase is untranslatable, but it conveys the sense that the faithful, having now received the Eucharist, are fittingly dis*miss*ed, or rather com*mission*ed, so that they may fulfill God's will in their daily lives. Saint Thomas Aquinas also suggested that the phrase *Ite missa est* refers to the priest "sending" the Eucharistic prayer to God, as in "The prayer is sent."

> And from this the mass derives its name *missa*; because the priest sends {*mittit*} his prayers up to God through the angel, as the people do through the priest. Or else because Christ is the victim sent {*missa*} to us: accordingly the deacon on festival days 'dismisses' the people at the end

of the mass, by saying: '*Ite, missa est*,' that is, the victim has been sent {*missa est*} to God through the angel, so that it may be accepted by God.[88]

In the Holy Sacrifice of the Mass, Christ is the sacrificial Lamb of God sent to God. As the Lamb of God, he is slain *and eaten*. Hence, the ritual of eating Christ is at the center of the Catholic Faith. Christ transforms the bread and wine of the Old Testament thanksgiving offering into His body and blood. It may seem even strange that Christ would desire for us to eat His flesh and blood. Yet we read: "Jesus said to them, 'Truly, truly, I say to you, unless you eat the flesh of the Son of man and drink his blood, you have no life in you'" (Jn 6:53). The act of eating Christ as the Lamb of God recalls the Jewish origins of the Catholic Church in the eternal plan of God.[89] Saint Paul makes it clear for us in his Second Epistle to the Corinthians:

> For Christ, our Passover Lamb has been sacrificed. Therefore, let us celebrate the feast, not with the old leaven, the leaven of malice and evil, but with the unleavened bread of sincerity and truth (2 Cor 5:7-8).[90]

Saint Paul identifies Jesus Christ as the true Passover Lamb of God. We might recall that when God delivered Moses and the Israelites out of Egypt, He did so by slaying the firstborn of Egypt. In order to protect the firstborn sons of Israel, God commanded that each Israelite family slay a lamb without blemish. Moses instructed that Israelites spread the blood of the lamb over the doorposts and lentils of their homes. When the angel of destruction visited the land of Egypt that night, the blood on the doorposts indicated that the plague should "pass over" the Israelite homes. Thus, the lamb was called the Passover lamb.

Jesus Christ is the true Passover Lamb of God. He is without blemish, which is to say, He is without sin. He was slain for our redemption and as Christ said at the Last Supper, His blood would be "poured out for many for the forgiveness of sins" (Mt 26:28). However, it was not enough for the ancient Israelites to merely slay the Passover lamb and place its blood over the doors of their homes. God's final instruction was that the lamb should be eaten by the entire family.

> Then they shall take some of the blood, and put it on the two doorposts and the lintel of the houses in which they eat them. They shall eat the flesh that night, roasted; with unleavened bread and bitter herbs they shall eat it (Ex 12:7-8).

The eating of the lamb signified that the family had become partakers of the redemption accomplished by God. Here we see that Paul's doctrine of redemptive participation hearkens back to the Old Covenant ritual of the Passover lamb. In fact, the eating of any sacrifice denotes that the recipient is a partaker of redemption. As we say—you are what you eat.

Our Lord Jesus Christ willed to fulfill His role as the unblemished Passover Lamb of God. Christ would be slain and His blood would be poured out for our redemption. Yet even more, it was necessary that Christ provide a way for His followers to partake in His sacrifice. A Passover would not be a Passover if the sacrificial lamb were not consumed by the family. The conclusion that Paul makes from Christ's identity as the Passover Lamb is astounding. Paul does not say, "Christ our Passover Lamb has been sacrificed, therefore let us accept Him as our Lord and Savior." No, Paul writes, "Christ, our Passover Lamb has been sacrificed. Therefore, let us celebrate the feast!" (2 Cor 5:7-8). The Apostle explains to the Christians in Corinth and to us today that since Christ the Passover Lamb has been sacrificed for us, it is necessary for us to celebrate the Passover feast. The implication is that this feast will entail eating the flesh of the Passover Lamb. The feast is the mysterious partaking of the body and blood of Christ. It is the Holy Eucharist. Just as the Israelites, year after year, partook of the redemption of their ancestors by ritually consuming the lamb for the feast of Passover, so Christians partake of Christ's redemption when we gather together for the Holy Sacrifice of the Mass. When we receive Holy Communion, the merits of Christ's life, death, and resurrection are applied to us and we are filled with the sanctifying grace of Christ's life. Saint Cyril explains, "The Word of God, united Himself to His own flesh, imparted to it a vivifying power, it became Him, therefore, to unite Himself to our bodies in a wonderful manner."[91]

NOTES

[75] *Didache*, 9, 1.

[76] Saint Justin Martyr, *First Apology* 1, 65-67; *Patrologia Graeca* 6, 428-429.

[77] Cf. Taylor Marshall, *The Crucified Rabbi: Judaism and the Origins of Catholic Christianity* (Dallas: Saint John Press, 2010).

[78] *Council of Trent*, Session 22, Chapter 1.

[79] *Council of Trent*, Session 22, Chapter 1.

[80] See the Douay-Rheims New Testament translation of 1 Corinthians 10:16: "The chalice of

benediction, which we bless, is it not the *communion* of the blood of Christ?" Incidentally, the Douay English translation of the New Testament was published in 1582—twenty-nine years before the publication of the Protestant "King James" Authorized Version of 1611.

[81] Saint Cyprian of Carthage, Epistle 62, 13.

[82] For a thorough treatment of Paul's separation of the Eucharistic rite from the Agape meal and the latter's relationship to the Jewish *chaburah* meal, see Dom Gregory Dix, *The Shape of the Liturgy* (New York: Continuum, 1945), 96-98.

[83] *Missale Romanum*, 2011 English Translation.

[84] ἀνάμνησις.

[85] See for example the Greek translation of Numbers 10:10: "On the day of your gladness also, and at your appointed feasts, and at the beginnings of your months, you shall blow the trumpets over your burnt offerings and over the sacrifices of your peace offerings; they shall serve you for remembrance {*anamnesis*} before your God: I am the Lord your God."

[86] *Council of Trent*, Session XIII, Chapter 4.

[87] For an example of Paul's Trinitarian theology, see 2 Corinthians 13:13: "The grace of our Lord Jesus Christ, and the charity of God, and the communication of the Holy Ghost be with you all. Amen."

[88] Saint Thomas Aquinas, *Summa theologiae* III, q. 83, a. 4.

[89] Taylor Marshall, *The Crucified Rabbi: Judaism and the Origins of Catholic Christianity* (Dallas, Texas: Saint John Press), 70-71.

[90] Translation mine.

NOTES CONTINUED

[91] Saint Cyril, *In Joan. (vi. 64)* lib. iv. c. 3.

8. PAUL ON THE PRIESTHOOD

…the priestly ministry of the Gospel of God…
ROMANS 15:16

…stewards of the mysteries of God…
1 CORINTHIANS 4:1

The One Priesthood of Christ: Two Participations

SAINT PAUL WAS A RABBI, an evangelist, a preacher, a
missionary, a minister, and an apostle—but was he a
priest? First, we must examine how a priest is different
from a minister or preacher. Certainly, priests preach
and teach, but they do more. Priests also mediate and
sacrifice on behalf of others. Since the New Testament
describes Christ as the great high priest of the New
Covenant, some have wrongly concluded that there are
no more priests in the New Testament, or that all
Christians are equally "priests" because each believer
has direct access to Christ. Following this argument,
there could not be any priests mediating between
believers and Christ, since Christ is the "one mediator
between God and man" (1 Tim 2:5). Since Christ
offered His sacrifice "once and for all" on the wood of
the cross, it would be inconceivable for any Christian to
offer *another* sacrifice. And yet, the Catholic Church
believes that there are ministerial priests who are distinct
from the laity and distinct from Christ. Why does the

Catholic Church believe this? The answer is that Saint Paul taught it. The key to understanding priesthood is to return to our constant theme of participation.

The Catholic Church holds that there are three kinds of priesthood, or rather, that there is the one priesthood of Christ and two participations within the one priesthood of Christ. Christ is without a doubt the High Priest of the New Covenant. "Since then we have a great high priest who has passed through the heavens, Jesus the Son of God, let us hold fast our confession" (Heb 4:14). However, Paul's doctrine of participation entails that the Christian faithful are participants in Christ's one priesthood in a relative way. We find this explicitly stated by Saint Peter:

> And like living stones be yourselves built into a spiritual house, to be a *holy priesthood*, to offer spiritual sacrifices acceptable to God through Jesus Christ...you are a chosen race, a *royal priesthood*, a holy nation, God's own people (1 Pet 2:5, 9).

Saint Paul also refers to this "priesthood of the believers" or "general priesthood of the baptized" in his epistle to the Romans: "I appeal to you therefore, brethren, by the mercies of God, to present your bodies as a living sacrifice, holy and acceptable to God, which is your reasonable act of worship" (Rom 12:1).[92] Christians are called upon to offer sacrifice to God. Like Christ, they offer their own bodies as a living sacrifice to the Father. Saint Paul assumes that this sacrifice offered by the individual Christian does not undermine the one sacrifice of Christ made at Calvary. Again, this is because the personal sacrifice of the Christian in worship is united to the one sacrifice of Christ through participation of the lesser within the greater. Following the teaching of Peter and Paul, the Catholic Church also officially teaches that the laity participates in this general priesthood of Christ. Pope Saint Leo the Great explained:

> For all those born again in Christ are made kings by the sign of the cross; they are consecrated priests by the oil of the Holy Spirit, so that beyond the special service of our ministry as priests, all spiritual and mature Christians know that they are a royal race and are sharers in the office of the priesthood."[93]

The identity of the laity as "priestly" is not entirely new with the New Covenant. The people of Israel in the Old Covenant were called "a kingdom of priests and a holy nation" (Ex 19:6; cf. Isa 61:6). Yet, God also chose one of the twelve tribes, the tribe of Levi, to engage in priestly service in a vocational manner. Thus, the ministerial *clerical* priesthood served the general *lay* priesthood of all Israel. These ministerial priests acted "on behalf of men in relation to God, to offer gifts and sacrifices for sins" (Heb 5:1).

Corresponding to the Old Covenant, there are also these two forms of priesthood. Through baptism and confirmation, the faithful are consecrated to be a holy priesthood. From this number, God also chooses men to minister to the faithful. These ordained men are the *ministerial* priests of the Catholic Church. These priests are not priests in their own right, but participate more deeply in the one priesthood of Christ. "Only Christ is the true priest," Thomas Aquinas wrote, "the others being only his ministers."[94]

As discussed in the previous chapter, the one sacrifice of Christ upon the cross was accomplished once for all. Nevertheless, the Holy Eucharist makes this same sacrifice present whenever and wherever the Holy Sacrifice of the Mass is celebrated. The same holds true for the one priesthood of Christ. The priesthood of Christ is made present through his ministerial priests on earth without diminishing the uniqueness of the high priesthood of Christ.

The one priesthood of Christ is therefore partaken of in two ways. The ministerial priesthood and the general priesthood both participate each in its own proper way in the one single priesthood of Christ. The Catholic Church teaches that although the ministerial priesthood and general priesthood are ordered to one another, they differ essentially.[95]

> While the common priesthood of the faithful is exercised by the unfolding of baptismal grace— a life of faith, hope, and charity, a life according to the Spirit, the ministerial priesthood is at the service of the common priesthood. It is directed at the unfolding of the baptismal grace of all Christians. The ministerial priesthood is a means by which Christ unceasingly builds up and leads his Church. For this reason it is transmitted by its own sacrament, the sacrament of Holy Orders.[96]

We find the same doctrine in Paul who describes his apostolic ministry as "priestly":

> But on some points I have written to you very boldly by way of reminder, because of the grace given me by God to be a minister of Christ Jesus to the Gentiles in the *priestly service* of the gospel of God, so that the offering of the Gentiles may be acceptable, sanctified by the Holy Spirit (Rom 15:15-16, *emphasis* mine).

Here the word translated as "minister" is the Greek word *leiturgon*—the same word from which we derive *liturgy*. The phrase "priestly service" is from the Greek word *hierourgounton*. It is derived from the Greek word *hiereus,* meaning "priest" or "sacrificer." It is the Greek word used to describe ministerial priests of the Old Covenant. Even if you do not know Greek, you can see how we derive the English word "hierarchy" from the Greek word *hiereus*. This single passage is loaded with priestly imagery. If we were to be overly literal, we might say that here Paul describes himself as a *liturgist* and as *priest!*

In another place, Saint Paul compares the ministerial priests of the New Covenant with the ministerial priests of the Old Covenant:

> Do you not know that those who are employed in the temple service get their food from the temple, and those who serve at the altar share in the sacrificial offerings? In the same way, the Lord commanded that those who proclaim the gospel should get their living by the Gospel (1 Cor 9:13-14).

In this passage, Paul clearly identifies New Covenant ministers with the same status awarded to Old Covenant priests. The implication is that New Covenant ministers are priests because they serve at the altar of God (cf. Heb 13:10).

Elsewhere, the office of apostle is identified with that of a priest: "Therefore, holy brethren, who share in a heavenly call, consider Jesus, the Apostle and High Priest of our confession" (Heb 3:1). Jesus Christ's identity as the chief apostle is the same as his identity as high priest. A passage in Luke stating that the Twelve Apostles "will eat and drink at my table in my kingdom,

and sit on thrones judging the twelve tribes of Israel"
(Lk 22:30) similarly depicts the Apostles in terms of
their royal priesthood. The Apostles then imparted this
ministerial priesthood to other men through the
sacrament of Holy Orders.

The Sacrament of Holy Orders

In multiple instances, we read of how the Apostles
conferred priestly authority on certain men by "the
laying on of hands." This is true also of the Apostle
Paul, who seems to have both received ordination by
laying on of hands (Gal 2:9; Acts 13:2-3), and to have
imposed his hands on the next generation of priests.
Consequently, the Catholic Church teaches that
ministerial priesthood is conferred by the sacrament of
Holy Orders, which in all cases entails the "laying on of
hands" by a Catholic bishop in apostolic succession.

Apostolic succession is the Catholic doctrine
stating that Christ ordained the twelve Apostles, who in
turn ordained men as bishops through the laying on of
hands. Those men then in turn ordained men by the
laying on of hands, and so on and so forth until we
arrive at the Catholic bishops of our time. Each Catholic
bishop can trace his apostolic succession back to the
Apostles through the laying on of hands. The purpose
of apostolic succession is to secure a sacramental chain
of grace in fulfillment of Saint Paul's words: "And what
you have heard from me before many witnesses entrust
to faithful men who will be able to teach others also" (2
Tim 2:2). The imposition of the bishop's hands in Holy
Orders signifies this act of entrusting the Apostolic
message to the next generation.

> Now the effects which must be produced and
> hence also signified by Sacred Ordination to the
> Diaconate, the Priesthood, and the Episcopacy,

namely power and grace, in all the rites of various times and places in the universal Church, are found to be sufficiently signified by the imposition of hands and the words which determine it.[97]

We find this sacrament of Holy Orders or the imposition of hands for the conferral of priesthood in several passages of the New Testament.

> These they set before the Apostles, and they prayed and laid their hands upon them (Acts 6:6).

Barnabas and Saul were consecrated through the laying on of hands:

> While the Apostles were worshiping the Lord and fasting, the Holy Spirit said, "Set apart for me Barnabas and Saul for the work to which I have called them." Then after fasting and praying they laid their hands on them and sent them off (Acts 13:2-3).

We read that Timothy had been consecrated as a bishop by Paul himself:

> Hence I remind you to rekindle the gift of God that is within you through the laying on of my hands (2 Tim 1:6).

This gift received in Holy Orders is an indelible spiritual character upon the soul of a priest that cannot be repeated or conferred temporarily. Once a man is ordained a priest, he is always a priest.

As is the custom today in the Catholic Church, all other priests join with the bishop in laying hands on the priestly candidate. Paul recalls this same ceremony in the priestly ordination of Timothy:

> Do not neglect the gift you have, which was given you by prophetic utterance when the council of presbyters laid their hands upon you (1 Tim 4:14).

And lastly Saint Paul commands Timothy to be careful in conferring the sacrament of Holy Orders upon other men:

> Do not be hasty in the laying on of hands, nor participate in another man's sins. Keep yourself pure (1 Tim 5:22).

As the passages above demonstrate, the Catholic Church's sacrament of Holy Orders through the laying on of hands is well established in the New Testament, but in particular in the writings of Saint Paul.

Bishops, Priests, and Deacons

We learn from the Acts of the Apostles, written by Paul's disciple Luke, and from the writings of Saint Paul that the hierarchy of the early Church was threefold. First, there were the Apostles. These men had unquestioned authority. Christ had promised to the Twelve: "He who receives you receives me, and he who receives me receives him who sent me" (Mt 10:40). Christ placed Peter as the leader of the Apostles:

> You are Peter {*Petros*}, and on this rock {*petra*} I will build my Church, and the gates of hell shall not prevail against it. I will give you the keys of the kingdom of heaven, and whatever you bind on earth shall be bound in heaven, and whatever

you loose on earth shall be loosed in heaven (Mt 16:18).

Thus, Peter and the Apostles formed the highest level of priestly authority in the Church.

The second level in the Church's hierarchy consisted of all those men who assisted the Apostles in the role of preaching the Gospel and administering the sacraments. We think of men like Mark, Luke, Silas, Timothy, and Titus. In the New Testament, these men are identified by either one of two Greek words. The first is the Greek word ἐπίσκοπος pronounced as *episcopos*. The word literally means "overseer." The word *episcopos* came into English as *piscop* or *biscop*, from which we derived the word *bishop*.

The second term used to describe the men who assisted the Apostles in their priestly duties is the Greek word πρεσβύτερος, pronounced as *presbyteros*. This word literally means "elder." The word *presbyteros* came into English as *prester*, from which we derive the word *priest*. Saint Paul speaks highly of the presbyters or priests of the Church:

> Let the presbyters who rule well be considered worthy of double honor, especially those who labor in preaching and teaching, for the scripture says, "You shall not muzzle an ox when it is treading out the grain," and, "The laborer deserves his wages" (1 Tim 5:17-18).

Saint Paul also instructed Titus, his appointed bishop of Crete, to appoint presbyters to minister in every town and villa:

> This is why I left you in Crete, that you might amend what was defective, and appoint

presbyters in every town as I directed you (Titus 1:5).

Without presbyters or priests, Paul considers the Church "defective."

On the third and lowest level of the Church's ministerial hierarchy were those whom the Apostles appointed with the intent that they take responsibility for the common duties of the Church.

> And the Twelve summoned the body of the disciples and said, "It is not right that we should give up preaching the word of God to serve tables. Therefore, brethren, pick out from among you seven men of good repute, full of the Spirit and of wisdom, whom we may appoint to this duty. But we will devote ourselves to prayer and to the ministry of the word." And what they said pleased the whole multitude, and they chose Stephen, a man full of faith and of the Holy Spirit, and Philip, and Prochorus, and Nicanor, and Timon, and Parmenas, and Nicolaus, a proselyte of Antioch. These they set before the Apostles, and they prayed and laid their hands upon them (Acts 6:1-6).

These seven common ministers came to be identified with the Greek word *diakonos*. The word means "servant," and came into English as *deacon*.

Thus, we can identify the entire hierarchy of the Catholic Church within the pages of the New Testament. The Pope is the successor of Saint Peter and he leads the apostolic college of the bishops. Under the bishops are the presbyters who minister in preaching and in celebrating the sacraments on the local level.

Lastly, there are the deacons who serve in ways so as to enable the bishops and priests to function more effectively.

At the time of the Protestant Reformation, many sought to undermine the threefold hierarchy of bishops, priests, and deacons by pointing out "bishops" and "presbyters" seemed to be the same office in the time of the Apostles. This we grant. However, after the Apostles died, those who took their place in Apostolic Succession reserved for themselves the title of "bishop," and the other ministers retained the title of "presbyter" or "priest." So it remains to this day.

Calling Priests "Father"

As a Protestant, I had been taught that the Catholics erred in calling their priests "father." After all, did not Christ say, "Call no man your father on earth, for you have one Father, who is in heaven" (Mt 23:9)? However, as time passed I came across several passages that seemed to contradict, or at least soften, the words of Christ. As I studied through the Acts of the Apostles, I read the following:

> And Stephen said: "Brethren and *fathers*, hear me. The God of glory appeared to our *father* Abraham…" (Acts 7:2).

Saint Stephen, just before he died, addressed the Jewish leaders as "brethren and fathers." We should remember that Paul, or rather Saul, was present on this occasion and was one of the "fathers" that Stephen had addressed. Clearly Stephen was not disobeying Christ when he called those men "fathers" or when he referred to Abraham as "father Abraham." Soon after, I observed that Scripture often refers to spiritual leaders as "fathers." Paul calls himself the "father" of the Christians in Corinth:

> For though you have countless guides in Christ, you do not have many fathers. For *I became your father in Christ Jesus* through the gospel. I urge you, then, be imitators of me (1 Cor 4:15-16).

Paul speaks this way individually of the recent convert Onesimus:

> I appeal to you for my child, Onesimus, *whose father I have become* in my imprisonment (Philem 10).

Moreover, Paul refers to his relationship with Timothy as that of a father and a son:

> But Timothy's worth you know, how *as a son with a father* he has served with me in the gospel (Phil 2:22).

If Stephen and Paul (and John for that matter, see 1 Jn 2:13-14) considered Christian ministry in terms of fatherhood, then what did Christ mean when He said, "Call no man your father on earth"?

Spiritual Fatherhood

Christ's condemnation of calling men "father" must be taken in the context with his condemnation of the "Scribes and Pharisees." The passage is worth citing in full:

> They bind heavy burdens, hard to bear, and lay them on men's shoulders; but they themselves will not move them with their finger. They do all

their deeds to be seen by men; for they make
their phylacteries broad and their fringes long,
and they love the place of honor at feasts and
the best seats in the synagogues, and salutations
in the market places, and being called rabbi by
men.

But you are not to be called *rabbi*, for you have
one teacher, and you are all brethren.

And call no man your *father* on earth, for you
have one Father, who is in heaven.

Neither be called *masters*, for you have one
master, the Christ…But woe to you, scribes and
Pharisees, hypocrites! because you shut the
kingdom of heaven against men; for you neither
enter yourselves, nor allow those who would
enter to go in (Mt 23:4-10, 13-14).

Christ condemns the scribes and Pharisees for three
sins. First, they create heavy burdens for their followers
and do not assist them spiritually. Second, they perform
great acts of piety in public, but they do not possess
faith. Third, they "shut the kingdom of heaven against
men." As a result, Christ condemns their hypocritical
audacity in assuming to bear three titles in particular:
father, rabbi, and master.

These three titles correspond to the three sins of
the scribes and Pharisees. First, they are hypocritical
spiritual "fathers" since they lay heavy burdens on their
followers. Fathers do not burden their children, but
assist them. Second, they are hypocrites by calling
themselves "rabbi," since they do not teach men, but
instead perform pious deeds in order to be seen by men.
Last of all, the scribes and Pharisees are hypocrites by

calling themselves "master" because it is the duty of a master to open and close his realm to those who belong to him. Instead, they "shut the kingdom of heaven against men."

The three sins listed by Christ correspond to these three titles, and so we come to see that Christ is not condemning the words *father*, *rabbi*, and *master*. Instead, Christ is saying, "Don't be a *father* in the way presumed by the hypocritical scribes and Pharisees. Don't be a *rabbi* in the way presumed by scribes and Pharisees. And don't be a *master* in the way presumed by the scribes and Pharisees."

Our intuition also tells us that Christ's words are not absolutely prohibitive. Do we not refer to our biological fathers as "fathers"? And yet if we literally interpret, "Call no man your father on earth," we would not even call our natural fathers by the title "father." Moreover, the word *rabbi* refers to a Jewish doctor of religious law. The word *rabbi* corresponds to the Latin word *doctor*, meaning an expert teacher. In Jewish culture, the term *rabbi* loosely corresponded to the modern equivalent of someone who has a Ph.D. Yet, we all call such men "Doctor." Even the English word *Mister* derives from *master* and yet we frequently refer to our superiors as *Mr. So-and-So*.

Christ used hyperbole to make his point against the behavior of the scribes and Pharisees. We find our Lord doing the same elsewhere: "If your right eye causes you to sin, pluck it out and throw it away; it is better that you lose one of your members than that your whole body be thrown into hell" (Mt 5:29). Obviously, we do not gouge out our eyes or amputate our limbs on account of sin. In the same way, Christ did not make an absolute prohibition against the use of the word *father*. Christ warns us against making a single guru the end all and be all of religion, instead of God Himself.

Beginning with Saint Peter, Catholic Christians look to the Pope for leadership, but all acknowledge that each individual pope is not the perennial authority for all time. Each pope dies and another takes his place. Christ's institution of the papacy (Mt 16:18), not an individual pope at a certain time, brings dignity to the Holy See.

Catholics call priests "father" because they see in them genuine spiritual fatherhood. Saint Paul lovingly referred to his priestly vocation as a task of spiritual fatherhood:

> For you know how, *like a father with his children*, we exhorted each one of you and encouraged you and charged you (1 Thess 2:11).

True spiritual fatherhood seeks to imitate God the Father in His love. It does not seek to replace the Father with its own authority. If a Catholic priest were to acquire the hypocritical spirit of the scribes and Pharisees and use his priesthood for his own self-interest, then the criticism of Christ would apply even to him.

Paul and Celibacy

Martin Luther and other Protestants were quick to point out that Paul seemed to tolerate married priests:

> Now a *bishop* must be above reproach, *the husband of one wife*, temperate, sensible, dignified, hospitable, an apt teacher (1 Tim 3:2).

And again in his correspondence with Titus:

> This is why I left you in Crete, that you might amend what was defective, and appoint *presbyters*

> in every town as I directed you, if any man is
> blameless, *the husband of one wife*, and his children
> are believers and not open to the charge of
> being profligate or insubordinate (Titus 1:6).

The Catholic Church grants this. In fact, the Catholic
Church does not dogmatically hold to priestly celibacy.
Nevertheless, celibacy is an ancient and revered custom
that denotes the radical commitment of a man who
desires to conform his life wholly to the life of Christ.
Let us not forget that the first celibate priest was Christ
Himself. There are certain exceptions to priestly celibacy
in the Catholic Church. The Eastern Catholic Churches
allow for married men (men married only once as Paul
instructs) to be ordained priests. However, even the
Eastern Church does not allow for priests to enter into
marriage once they have become priests. It is safe to say
that it would be extremely scandalous to see your parish
priest dating women in the parish or seeking to become
engaged!

The significance of Paul's peculiar rule that
bishops and presbyters be "the husband of one wife" is
often neglected. Christian Cochini, in his monumental
work *The Apostolic Origins of Priestly Celibacy,* has
convincingly demonstrated that clerical celibacy was
already the norm in the generation of the Apostles.[98]
Peter no doubt was married—Matthew, Mark, and Luke
each mention Peter's mother-in-law.[99] Nevertheless, all
those after the very first generation of Apostles were
celibate. John, the youngest Apostle, was celibate. Paul
was celibate. Luke was celibate. Barnabas was celibate.
Timothy was celibate. Titus was celibate. Mark was
celibate. The earliest known bishops ordained by the
Apostles—Clement of Rome, Polycarp of Smyrna, and
Ignatius of Antioch—were also celibates. Besides Peter,
it is difficult to find any documentation of married

clergy in the first two centuries of Christianity. Instead, we find celibate clergy everywhere.

Cochini does find instances in which married men were ordained in the early centuries of the Church. However, he demonstrates that they were either widowers or had given up sexual relations in order to focus their attention to the mission at hand. As Saint Paul reminded Timothy, "No soldier on service gets entangled in civilian pursuits, since his aim is to satisfy the one who enlisted him" (2 Tim 2:4). Saint Paul's stipulation that a bishop or presbyter be *the husband of one wife* is either a concession made in the earliest times of the Church, since most adult male converts would have been married men, or it presumes continence on the part of these married men. Cochini identifies the condition of *one wife* as a signal that such men have mastered their sexual desires, since they are not serial monogamists, marrying one woman after another. If the bishop or priest's wife should die, he would then be less tempted to seek another wife. He would at this point enter into the celibate state with the rest of the clergy.

In any case, the Catholic preference for priestly celibacy is strongly made elsewhere by Saint Paul himself:

> It is well for a man not to touch a woman. But because of the temptation to immorality, each man should have his own wife and each woman her own husband. The husband should give to his wife her conjugal rights, and likewise the wife to her husband. For the wife does not rule over her own body, but the husband does; likewise the husband does not rule over his own body, but the wife does. Do not refuse one another except perhaps by agreement for a season, that you may devote yourselves to

> prayer; but then come together again, lest Satan tempt you through lack of self-control.
>
> I say this by way of concession, not of command. I wish that all were as I myself am. But each has his own special gift from God, one of one kind and one of another (1 Cor 7:1-7).

Paul teaches that it is well for a man not to touch a woman. This is the Pauline presupposition of every Catholic priest of the Roman rite. Paul himself even wishes that all Christians "were as I myself am." In other words, Paul thinks very highly of his celibate state. Yet, Paul also realizes that it is not for everyone, because "each one has his own special gift from God."

Paul's reference to this "special gift" recalls Christ's words encouraging the existence of "eunuchs for the kingdom of heaven," eunuchs being those who neither marry nor have intercourse:

> For there are eunuchs who have been so from birth, and there are eunuchs who have been made eunuchs by men, and there are eunuchs who have made themselves eunuchs for the sake of the kingdom of heaven. He who is able to receive this, let him receive it (Mt 19:22).

Christ teaches that some are "able to receive this." In other words, it is a spiritual gift that assists in the building up of the kingdom of heaven. Saint Paul, following this instruction of Christ, seeks to encourage the vocation of spiritual eunuchs:

> Are you bound to a wife? Do not seek to be free. Are you free from a wife? Do not seek marriage. But if you marry, you do not sin, and

> if a girl marries she does not sin. Yet those who
> marry will have worldly troubles, and I would
> spare you that (1 Cor 7:27-28).

Marriage is not a sin. As we shall see in the next chapter,
marriage is a sacrament. It is a magnificent blessing and
it signifies the union between Christ and the Church.
Nevertheless, marriage does bring with it "worldly
troubles," as Paul explains:

> The unmarried man is anxious about the affairs
> of the Lord, how to please the Lord, but the
> married man is anxious about worldly affairs,
> how to please his wife, and his interests are
> divided (1 Cor 7:33-34).

Paul teaches that, all things being equal, a celibate man
is able to devote more energy to "the affairs of the
Lord" and the married man is "more anxious about
worldly affairs." The married man must rightfully
concern himself with his relationship with his wife and
children, with his own mortgage, bills, college funds,
and retirement plan. The celibate man lives, for the
most part, without these cares, and as Paul says, "he is
anxious about the affairs of the Lord." Having stated
this, Paul summarizes his position on celibacy and
marriage:

> So that he who marries his betrothed does well;
> and he who refrains from marriage will do better
> (1 Cor 7:38).

Briefly stated, Paul teaches: "Marriage is great. Celibacy
is greater." Saint Paul and the Catholic Church
recognize in the words of Christ concerning "eunuchs
for the kingdom of heaven" that celibacy is a unique gift

that allows certain Christians to dedicate themselves to God in a remarkable way. Nevertheless, the Catholic Church teaches that all Christians are called to live a life of chastity: "Married people are called to live conjugal chastity; others practice chastity in continence."[100] Within the Catholic Church, married couples are by no means second-class Christians. They also contribute to the spiritual well-being of the Church. There are countless married saints whose lives are celebrated alongside those saints who were celibates. As Saint Ambrose once said:

> There are three forms of the virtue of chastity: the first is that of spouses, the second that of widows, and the third that of virgins. We do not praise any one of them to the exclusion of the others.[101]

With these words, let us turn to Saint Paul's words concerning the sacrament of marriage.

NOTES

[92] Translation mine.

[93] Saint Leo the Great, *Sermo* 4, 1-2 (*Patrologia Latina* 54, 148-149).

[94] Thomas Aquinas, *Commentary on the Epistle to the Hebrews* 8, 4.

[95] *Lumen Gentium* 10, 2.

[96] *Catechism of the Catholic Church* §1547.

[97] *Pope Pius XII, Sacramentum Ordinis (On the Sacrament of Order),* Apostolic Constitution of 1947.

[98] Christian Cochini, *The Apostolic Origins of Priestly Celibacy* (San Francisco: Ignatius Press, 1990).

NOTES CONTINUED

[99] Mt 8:14-15, Mk 1:29-34, Lk 4:38-39.

[100] *Catechism of the Catholic Church* §2349.

[101] Saint Ambrose of Milan, *On Widows* 4, 23 (*Patrologia Latina* 16, 255A).

9. PAUL ON HOLY MATRIMONY AS SACRAMENT

…this is a great mystery…
EPHESIANS 5:32

Marriage as a Sacrament

THE CATHOLIC CHURCH HOLDS marriage to be a sacrament. This conviction derives from the fact that human sexuality was rightly and properly established by God in the book of Genesis, and that the union of husband and wife points to the final "Wedding Supper of the Lamb" as described in the book of Revelation. In the book of Genesis we read, "So God created man in his own image, in the image of God he created him; male and female he created them" (Gen 1:27). As a result, there are very few examples of celibates in the Old Testament, though Elijah, Jeremiah, and John the Baptist come to mind. The reason for this is that God established his covenant with Abraham as being fulfilled through procreation:

> I will indeed bless you, and I will multiply your descendants as the stars of heaven and as the sand that is on the seashore (Gen 22:17).

The purpose of marriage and procreation was to establish the holy nation of Israel in which the Messiah would be born of the Virgin Mary. Even Christ was born in the household of a married couple, though Christ's incarnation did not depend on the natural means of procreation. In Mary and Joseph we find the nexus of the Old Covenant and the New Covenant. We also find the nexus of marriage and celibacy.

In the previous chapter, we observed how Paul exhorted some Christians to embrace celibacy as it pertained to the supernatural order. Paul certainly did not forbid marriage. In fact, Saint Paul condemned those first-century Christians who forbade the sacrament of marriage on grounds that it was somehow unclean:

> Now the Spirit expressly says that in later times some will depart from the faith by giving heed to deceitful spirits and doctrines of demons, through the pretensions of liars whose consciences are seared, who forbid marriage and enjoin abstinence from foods which God created to be received with thanksgiving by those who believe and know the truth (1 Tim 4:1-3).

For Paul and the Catholic Church, the supernatural order does not replace or destroy the natural order. Rather, as Saint Thomas Aquinas articulated, "grace perfects nature."[102] Christian enthusiasm for celibacy by no means denigrates marriage. As the epistle to the Hebrews states, "Let marriage be held in honor among all" (Heb 13:4). Saint Luke, Paul's disciple, preserving the words of Christ, distinguishes marriage as pertaining to the natural order from celibacy as it pertains to the supernatural order.

And Jesus said to them, "The sons of this age marry and are given in marriage; but those who are accounted worthy to attain to that age and to the resurrection from the dead neither marry nor are given in marriage" (Lk 20:34-35).

Our Lord teaches that marriage will not exist in heaven. All will live as celibates for eternity, since marriage points to the final union between Christ and His Church. Once God has accomplished the perfect union of Christ and the Catholic Church, the sacrament of marriage is no longer necessary. This is why wedding vows end with "Until death do us part." The death of one spouse brings the marriage bond to an end.

Marriage as an Icon of Christ with the Church

Catholic tradition assigns great importance to Christ's presence at the wedding of Cana (Jn 2:1-11). The presence of Jesus and Mary at this wedding confirms the goodness of marriage and reveals that Christ not only approves of marriage, but also blesses the marital bond and "elevated it to the dignity of a Sacrament."[103] The virginity of Christ and the virginity of Mary, both present at the wedding in Cana, do not nullify the institution of marriage, but rather uphold it. Saint John Chrysostom makes the same observation:

> Whoever denigrates marriage also diminishes the glory of virginity. Whoever praises it makes virginity more admirable and resplendent. What appears good only in comparison with evil would not be truly good. The most excellent good is something even better than what is admitted to be good.[104]

The Church esteems voluntary celibacy because she so highly esteems marriage. Celibacy can only be rightly appreciated when one realizes that it is a sacrifice of some great good.

Saint Paul confirms the greatness of marriage within the Church in his epistle to the Ephesians. Paul first cites the book of Genesis and then makes a profound statement:

> "For this reason a man shall leave his father and mother and be joined to his wife, and the two shall become one flesh." *This is a great mystery*, and I am saying that *it refers to Christ and the Church* because we are members of His Body (Eph 5:28-30).

The Latin Vulgate renders Paul's Greek word *mystery* as "sacrament." The Latin Vulgate translation of this passage reads: *sacramentum hoc magnum est* or "This is a great sacrament!" The Apostle Paul teaches that marriage is a great sacrament because it is an icon of the final union between Christ and the Church. Once again, we find Paul's doctrine of participation applied to marriage. The husband and wife, as "members of His Body," become a living icon of the mysterious union between Christ and His Church.

A husband and wife who have a self-serving and disagreeable marriage do a great disservice to their children and to the greater community. Whether they know it or not, they are portraying the union of Christ and His Church as one of tension rather than harmony. On the other hand, a couple that lives according to the sacramental grace of matrimony, husband and wife offering themselves as a gift to the other, such a couple properly mirrors the reality of Christ's love for the Church and the Church's love for Christ. A beautiful marriage proclaims the beauty of the Gospel. For this reason, marriage is a great mystery.

The Roles of Husband and Wife

Let it be said that Saint Paul's description of marital roles is controversial. The Apostle certainly does not establish specific duties, such as which spouse should take out the garbage. Instead, he proposes an overarching principle of behavior that roots itself in the love of Christ.

> For the husband is the head of the wife as Christ is the head of the Church, His Body, and is Himself its Savior. As the Church is subject to Christ, so let wives also be subject in everything to their husbands (Eph 5:23-24).

From these words, we observe that Paul is neither a progressive egalitarian nor a secular feminist. Paul cannot be pigeonholed in this way because he defines marital roles *in accord with his Christology*. The secular world will never understand Paul's doctrine of marriage because it does not understand Christ. If a person does not understand Christ's crucified love, then he will not understand marital love, because Paul roots marital love in sacrifice. It is true that the husband is the "head of the wife as Christ is the head of the Church." We can hear an army of feminists balk at this so-called oppressive and patriarchal jargon. Yet, Christ is not a Persian emperor who reigns from an enclosed temple over his distant subjects. Christ is "God with us," and He demonstrated His love for us upon the cross. Saint Paul writes:

> Husbands, love your wives, as Christ loved the Church and gave Himself up for her, that He

> might sanctify her, having cleansed her by the washing of water with the word (Eph 5:25-26).

How did Christ love His Church? He endured betrayal, false accusation, ridicule, scourging, hunger, exhaustion, and finally the span of several hours nailed to a cross in the noonday heat. Could any love be greater? Would any woman object to this sort of devotion? Secular feminists protest against Christian gender roles because they have not observed authentic manhood performed in the pattern of Christ.

If Paul were alive today and the Christian husband should ask the Apostle for a job description of husbandry, the Apostle might merely hand a crucifix to him and say, "Study this." For within the contours of the crucified Christ we find what it means to be a husband. To be a husband is to be a man who sacrifices himself for his wife. He suffers for his wife. Furthermore, he sanctifies her "by the washing of water with the word." This is a clear reference to baptism, the means by which Christ incorporates us into His Church. By this we learn that the husbands should be the spiritual warriors of the Christian family.

Paul would not be content to see pious wives bearing the brunt of religious education for themselves and for their children. Paul expects that Christian fathers take the charge for the religious education of their children: "Fathers, do not provoke your children to anger, but bring them up in the discipline and instruction of the Lord" (Eph 6:4). I might even go so far as to say that the Catholic Church in America has experienced a shortage of vocations to the priesthood because young men are unwilling to pursue spiritual fatherhood on account of the absence of real fatherhood in their own homes.

Turning to Christian wives, Paul states, "As the Church is subject to Christ, so let wives also be subject in everything to their husbands" (Eph 5:24). If the husband loved his wife as the crucified Lord loved the Church, would any woman object to Paul's exhortation? Do pious Catholic Christians mope about because they are "subject to Christ"? On the contrary, we are quite glad to be subject to Christ. It is only fitting that we follow Christ, because Christ has our best interests at heart. The same is true for Christian husbands and wives. Saint Paul goes on to explain:

> Even so husbands should love their wives as their own bodies. He who loves his wife loves himself. For no man ever hates his own flesh, but nourishes and cherishes it, as Christ does the Church (Eph 5:28-29).

Paul expects that Christian husbands will love their wives with all their strength. We may find it difficult to fulfill Paul's elevated view of marriage. In our time, when cohabitation and divorce are commonly accepted, we see that sacramental grace is in fact necessary for a successful marriage. Marriage that lacks the Pauline doctrine of self-offering and self-sacrifice is doomed to fail. This is why the Catholic Church defends the sacramental status of matrimony against those who deny it. According to the Council of Trent (1545-1563), the sacrament of holy matrimony confers:

> the grace which might perfect that natural love, and confirm that indissoluble union, and sanctify the married, Christ Himself, the institutor and perfecter of the venerable sacraments, merited for us by His passion.[105]

166 THE CATHOLIC PERSPECTIVE ON PAUL

The grace received through the sacrament of holy matrimony perfects natural love and actually sanctifies us. It is the grace "merited for us by His passion." When a married Christian couple cooperates with this grace, they each become more holy. In other words, they are ushered along the path of salvation.

The Prohibition against Divorce and Remarriage

Even more controversial is Saint Paul's doctrine against divorce. Following Saint Paul, the Catholic Church identifies marriage as *indissoluble* because the sacrament of marriage cannot be *dissolved* in this life. This stipulation follows the teaching that Christ gave in the Sermon on the Mount

> But I say to you that every one who divorces his wife, except on the ground of unchastity, makes her an adulteress; and whoever marries a divorced woman commits adultery (Mt 5:32).

When at another time Christ was asked about the indissolubility of marriage, Christ responded:

> The two shall become one flesh. So they are no longer two but one flesh. What therefore God has joined together, let no man put asunder (Mk 10:8-9).

His disciples once again asked Christ on the matter and he responded yet again:

> Whoever divorces his wife and marries another, commits adultery against her; and if she divorces her husband and marries another, she commits adultery (Mk 10:11-12).

Consider this. If God has joined together a baptized man and a baptized woman in the holy *sacrament* of matrimony so that they are "no longer two but one flesh," how can they be separated? Rightly does Christ proclaim, "What therefore God has joined together, let no man put asunder." A state court or a minister cannot separate what God has joined. This is why Saint Paul teaches that the bond of matrimony is sacred and indissoluble.

Christ's teaching surpasses the Old Testament teaching of Moses. Moses allowed the Israelites to divorce their wives. A certificate of divorce was issued to the wife and both spouses were free to remarry. This practice was a concession to human sin and the lack of grace available through the Old Covenant. As Christ taught, "For your hardness of heart Moses allowed you to divorce your wives, but from the beginning it was not so" (Mt 19:8).

> In his preaching Jesus unequivocally taught the original meaning of the union of man and woman as the Creator willed it from the beginning; permission given by Moses to divorce one's wife was a concession to the hardness of hearts. The matrimonial union of man and woman is indissoluble: God himself has determined it "what therefore God has joined together, let no man put asunder."[106]

Christ returns marriage to its glorious state as originally intended by God. One can hardly imagine a divorce between Adam and Eve in the Garden of Eden. The impossibility of Christian divorce in the New Covenant is accounted for by the fact that Christ the Lord elevated marriage between the baptized to the dignity of a sacrament."[107]

Let me interject at this point that not all marriages are sacramental marriages. For instance, the Catholic Church holds that marriages ratified by a justice of the peace or by a secular court are not in fact *sacramental* marriages. Christian marriage entails vows before God and the purpose of imitating the union of Christ and the Church. Hence, Catholic weddings are liturgical acts of worship regulated by the Church for the greater glory of God. Consequently, the Catholic Church distinguishes between the secular "matrimonial contracts" on the one hand, and the spiritual "sacramental marriages" on the other.[108] The former may be dissolved on account of the so-called Petrine and Pauline privileges. The latter may not be dissolved, because sacramental marriages have been ratified by God from heaven. "What God has joined together, let no man put asunder."

In order for a marriage to be an indissoluble *sacramental marriage*, the Catholic Church's *Code of Canon Law* stipulates that it must be celebrated under the canonical norms of the Church and both parties must intentionally consent to what the Catholic Church articulates as the sacrament of marriage. Furthermore, there are certain *diriment impediments* that render a marriage null and void. "A diriment impediment renders a person unqualified to contract marriage validly."[109] Examples of diriment impediments would be violations of the law of consanguinity, such as marrying your sister (Canon 1091), or attempting to enter into marriage with someone who is either underage or insane (Canons 1083 & 1095). For those interested, a full treatment of this subject is given in the Catholic Church's *Code of Canon Law* (1983), canons 1055-1165.

Saint Paul assumes rather matter-of-factly in his epistle to the Romans that sacramental marriages are indissoluble:

Thus a married woman is bound by law to her husband as long as he lives; but if her husband dies she is discharged from the law concerning the husband. Accordingly, she will be called an adulteress if she lives with another man while her husband is alive. But if her husband dies she is free from that law, and if she marries another man she is not an adulteress (Rom 7:2-3).

Paul states that a divorced woman becomes an adulteress if she marries another man while her husband still lives. Her sacramental bond to the first husband remains even if she herself rejects it. This is a faithful interpretation of Christ's words, "What God has joined together, let no man put asunder." Paul affirms the same once again when writing to the Christians in Corinth:

To the married I give charge, not I but the Lord, that the wife should not separate from her husband, but if she does, let her remain single or else be reconciled to her husband—and that the husband should not divorce his wife (1 Cor 7:10-11).

Saint Paul realizes that marriage partners may wish to separate for one reason or another. Sadly, the betrayal of adultery, physical abuse, and other such sins can deeply damage the love between two people who have been united in sacramental marriage.

In such cases the Church permits the physical separation of the couple and their living apart. The spouses do not cease to be husband and wife before God and so are not free to contract a new union. In this difficult situation, the best

> solution would be, if possible, reconciliation. The Christian community is called to help these persons live out their situation in a Christian manner and in fidelity to their marriage bond which remains indissoluble.[110]

Unfortunately in a culture plagued by divorce and remarriage, many people who have entered into indissoluble and sacramental unions have already made recourse to civil divorce. In such cases, the Catholic Church must continue to recognize their original sacramental marriages:

> The Church maintains that a new union cannot be recognized as valid, if the first marriage was valid. If the divorced are remarried civilly, they find themselves in a situation that objectively contravenes God's law...The remarriage of persons divorced from a living, lawful spouse contravenes the plan and law of God as taught by Christ. They are not separated from the Church, but they cannot receive Eucharistic communion. They will lead Christian lives especially by educating their children in the faith.[111]

Because the Lord Jesus Christ and Saint Paul clearly forbid the remarriage of those who have been sacramentally married to a person still alive, the Catholic Church must also maintain this teaching.

NOTES

[102] Saint Thomas Aquinas, *Summa theologiae* I, q. 62, a. 5.

NOTES CONTINUED

[103] Ludwig Ott, *Fundamentals of Catholic Dogma*, 463.

[104] Saint John Chrysostom, *On Virginity* 10, 1: *Patrologia Graeca* 48, 540.

[105] *Council of Trent*, Session 24, "Doctrine of the Sacrament of Matrimony."

[106] *Catechism of the Catholic Church* §1614.

[107] Ott, *Fundamentals*, 463.

[108] *Code of Canon Law* (1983), Canon 1055 §2. "For this reason, a valid matrimonial contract cannot exist between the baptized without it being by that fact a sacrament."

[109] *Code of Canon Law* (1983), Canon 1073.

[110] *Catechism of the Catholic Church* §1649.

[111] *Catechism of the Catholic Church* §1650, §1665.

10. Paul on Human Sexuality

...for this is the will of God, your sanctification:
that you abstain from unchastity...
1 THESSALONIANS 4:3

IN OUR DAY, Saint Paul is most maligned for his so-called stodgy moral principles. The so-called progressive lobbies stand in lockstep opposition to the moral principles articulated by Saint Paul. As observed in the previous chapter, Paul opposes a culture that revels in no-fault divorce. Paul also stands against homosexuality, feminist theology, pornography, pre-marital sex, "living together," abortion, and yes, contraception. For all of Paul's emphasis on grace and freedom, he also sets down the narrow pathway by which we reach true freedom.

Extra-Marital Sexual Intercourse

If you look in a Bible concordance for the phrase "pre-marital sex" you will find nothing. That is because ancient Jews thought of sexual intercourse as either rightly exercised *within* the bonds of matrimony or wrongly exercised *outside* the bonds of matrimony. Western culture once observed a similar ideal and employed a catalogue of terms to describe the various sexual aberrations. Sexual intercourse that occurred between an unmarried man and an unmarried woman was called "fornication." Sexual intercourse in which at least one partner was married to another party was called "adultery." The practice of a man and woman living together outside the bond of marriage is today called "living together." Previously it was known as the sin of "concubinage." It was in fact worse than fornication because it publicly flaunted moral decency.

In antiquity, sexual norms were observed for a number of reasons. First of all, public opinion regarding sexual matters affected one's social standing. If a young lady possessed a reputation of promiscuity, she might as well give up all hopes of becoming married. Secondly, children born outside of wedlock were considered illegitimate, even "bastards." Such children were born in disgrace and were without legal inheritance in most cases. Thirdly, marriage served as the glue of society. To break these bonds through sexual immorality was seen as an attack upon the social order. Moreover, inheritance laws depended upon the certainty of heirs. The only way to secure the identity of heirs is to observe sexual norms.

In seeking to secure sexual purity in the early Church, Saint Paul did not appeal to social conventions. Paul's rationale is based on the fact that the Christian believer participates in the life Christ, and this mystical reality renders sexual impurity as repugnant.

> The body is not meant for immorality, but for the Lord, and the Lord for the body. And God raised the Lord and will also raise us up by his power. Do you not know that your bodies are members of Christ? Shall I therefore take the members of Christ and make them members of a prostitute? Never! Do you not know that he who joins himself to a prostitute becomes one body with her? (1 Cor 6:13-16)

The Christian is a member of Christ through baptism. Since he is joined to Christ, how then can he join himself with a prostitute? Paul brings his doctrine of the Church to bear upon his moral instructions. Paul continues to emphasize the incompatibility of sexual immorality with the believer's participation in Christ.

> Shun immorality. Every other sin which a man commits is outside the body; but the immoral man sins against his own body. Do you not know that your body is a temple of the Holy Spirit within you, which you have from God? You are not your own. You were bought with a price. So glorify God in your body (1 Cor 6:18-20).

The physical body of the Christian is a temple of the Holy Spirit. It is holy and unworthy of unlawful interactions. Paul emphasizes the sacredness of the body to cast light on the filthiness of sexual immorality. For this reason Paul writes to the Christians in Ephesus:

> But fornication and all impurity or covetousness must not even be named among you, as is fitting among saints (Eph 5:3).

Saint Paul lays down the principle "become what you are in Christ, that is, holy." Through their union with Christ, Christians are holy, and so they must be holy. For this reason, Saint Paul asserts:

> For this is the will of God, your sanctification: that you abstain from unchastity; that each one of you know how to take a wife for himself in holiness and honor, not in the passion of lust like heathen who do not know God; that no

> man transgress, and wrong his brother in this
> matter, because the Lord is an avenger in all
> these things, as we solemnly forewarned you.
> For God has not called us for uncleanness, but
> in holiness (1 Thess 4:3-7).

For Paul, our call to holiness is bound up in the
preservation of purity in marriage, not in the lust of the
heathen. Christians should stand out in their steadfast
commitment to sexual purity in all ways.

Homosexuality

One afternoon while ministering to the homeless in
downtown Fort Worth, Texas, I fell into a conversation
with a stranger about religion, which eventually led to
the subject of Christ. Without hesitating, he came right
out and said, "I'm a gay Christian." After he admitted to
being an active homosexual, he added, "I have studied
the whole Bible and nowhere does it teach that
homosexuality is a sin." I countered his claim, but the
conversation became understandably awkward.

Since then, I've met others who believe that the
Bible does not condemn homosexual acts as sinful. In
fact, the Apostle Paul condemned homosexuality on
three separate occasions. In his epistle to the Romans,
Paul describes the origin of idolatry and associates it
with the origins of homosexuality, among both men and
women:

> Their women exchanged natural relations for
> unnatural, and the men likewise gave up natural
> relations with women and were consumed with
> passion for one another, men committing
> shameless acts with men and receiving in their
> own persons the due penalty for their error. And
> since they did not see fit to acknowledge God,

God gave them up to a base mind and to improper conduct (Rom 1:26-28).

Paul identifies homosexuality with the following terms: unnatural, shameless acts, error, base mind, and improper conduct.

Saint Paul also explains that practicing homosexuals "will not inherit the kingdom of God":

> Do you not know that the unrighteous will not inherit the kingdom of God? Do not be deceived; neither the immoral, nor idolaters, nor adulterers, nor effeminates {*malakoi*}, nor homosexuals {*arsenokoitai*}, nor thieves, nor the greedy, nor drunkards, nor revilers, nor robbers will inherit the kingdom of God (1 Cor 6:9-10).

The words translated as "effeminates" and "homosexuals" are often omitted in modern Bible translations and replaced with the single word "perverts," even though two separate words appear in the Greek text of Paul's First Epistle to the Corinthians.[112] One might understand why the man I met in Fort Worth believed that "homosexuality was not condemned in the Bible," since many English versions actually hide the term under pretence of translation. The two Greek words used by Paul in this passage are *malakoi* and *arsenokoitai*. The word *malakoi* is sometimes translated *effeminate*s and the word *arsenokoitai* is translated as *homosexuals*.

The Greek word *arsenokoitai* undoubtedly refers to male homosexuality. The very etymology of the word *arsenokoitai* reveals this. It is a compound of two words: *arsen* meaning "male" and *koitai* meaning "bed," and specifically "marriage bed."[113] Thus, *arsenokoitai* literally means "men in bed together."

Lest there be any doubt about the identity of *arsenokoitai* with homosexuals, let us turn to the Greek Septuagint version of Leviticus 20:13, which reads, "If a man lies with a male as with a woman, both of them have committed an abomination; they shall be put to death."[114] While the Old Testament death penalty for homosexuality was abolished by Christ, this passage undoubtedly refers to homosexual practice and confirms that Paul's use of the Greek word *arsenokoitai* prohibits the same behavior described in Leviticus 20:13—men having relations with men. The Greek Septuagint renders this passage as: *kai hos an koimethe meta arsenos koiten gynaikos.* We find within it the same two Greek words that compose the word *arsenokoitai,* which was used by Paul to condemn homosexuality. I have underlined the words above to make the connection more obvious. Here we see *arsonos* and *koiten* together describing homosexual activity in the clear language of Leviticus 20:13. Clearly, Paul's use of the similar compound word *arsenokoitai* refers to homosexual men—men in bed with other men.

The word used by Saint Paul, *malakoi,* literally means "soft ones." There are three interpretations as to what this term might mean. First, it may refer to those who are overly obsessed with luxury, an attribute that would have been identified with effeminacy in antiquity. The second interpretation is one given by the Jewish historian Josephus. Josephus identifies *soft ones* with men who dressed as women and sometimes even mutilated or removed their male genitals.[115] These men may have been the passive partners in homosexual acts in the context of pagan ritual festivals, i.e. cultic male prostitutes. However, we must grant that the term *malakoi* is not explicitly used in this regard. The third possible solution is the one given by Saint Thomas Aquinas, which states that the "sin of softness" is the sin of masturbation.[116] Incidentally, the Catholic Church considers masturbation as sin against chastity:

> masturbation is an intrinsically and gravely disordered action. The deliberate use of the sexual faculty, for whatever reason, outside of marriage is essentially contrary to its purpose.[117]

If Paul intended to refer to masturbation in his condemnation of "soft ones," then he stands in agreement with the Church's condemnation of masturbation. Whatever Paul meant by *soft ones*, it seems to have pertained to sexual sin, since in Paul's list it falls between adultery and homosexuality.

The third passage in which Paul condemns homosexuality is found in his First Epistle to Timothy where he identifies homosexuals as lawless and disobedient:

> The law is not made for the just man, but for the unjust and disobedient, for the ungodly and sinners, for the wicked and defiled, for murderers of fathers and murderers of mothers, for manslayers, fornicators, homosexuals {*arsenokoitai*}, kidnapers, liars, perjurers, and whatever else is contrary to sound doctrine (1 Tim 1:9-10).

Once again, the original Greek word used here by Paul for *homosexuals* is the same word that he used before: *arsenokoitai*. Clearly, Saint Paul was opposed to homosexual acts. The Catholic Church conforms to Paul in this regard:

> Basing itself on Sacred Scripture, which presents homosexual acts as acts of grave depravity,

> tradition has always declared that "homosexual acts are intrinsically disordered." They are contrary to the natural law. They close the sexual act to the gift of life. They do not proceed from a genuine affective and sexual complementarity. Under no circumstances can they be approved.[118]

Nevertheless, the Catholic Church recognizes that,

> The number of men and women who have deep-seated homosexual tendencies is not negligible. This inclination, which is objectively disordered, constitutes for most of them a trial. They must be accepted with respect, compassion, and sensitivity.

> Homosexual persons are called to chastity. By the virtues of self-mastery that teach them inner freedom, at times by the support of disinterested friendship, by prayer and sacramental grace, they can and should gradually and resolutely approach Christian perfection.[119]

Abortion and Contraception

The Catholic Christian tradition is unwavering in its opposition to abortion. This opposition is based on the conviction that the newly conceived child is a human person from the moment of his or her conception. Sacred Scripture repeatedly affirms the personhood of the unborn child.

> For thou didst form my inward parts, thou didst knit me together in my mother's womb (Ps 139:13-16).

> Before I formed you in the womb I knew you,
> and before you were born I consecrated you (Jer
> 1:5).

Saint Paul also provides a convincing passage where he
testifies to his own personhood prior to being born:

> But when he who had set me apart before I was
> born, and had called me through his grace (Gal
> 1:15).

Saint Paul's close disciple, Saint Luke, testified to the
personhood of the unborn John the Baptist:

> The baby leapt in her womb (Lk 1:41).

Since direct abortion seeks to destroy the life of children
before they are born, the Church considers abortion to
be a grave sin. "It decrees excommunication, that is,
deprivation of the Sacraments and of the Prayers of the
Church in the case of any of her members, and other
privations besides in the case of clergymen—against all
who seek to procure abortion, if their action produces
the effect."[120]

Several ancient Christian documents testify to
the sinfulness of abortion. The *Didache*, a late first-
century Christian document, states, "Thou shalt do no
sorcery, thou shalt not murder a child by abortion nor
kill them when born."[121] This passage not only
condemns abortion by name, but it also links it with
"sorcery." This translation of the word "sorcery" is
somewhat misleading. The Greek word is *pharmakeuseis*.
It is the word from which we derive the English word
pharmaceutical or *pharmacy*. It refers to the art of making
drugs. In antiquity this task had been identified with
"sorcery." We might think of a witchdoctor who

concocts magical potions. These witchdoctors or "pharmacists" were known primarily for being able to create potions or drugs that would make a woman sterile or induce the abortion of a child already conceived. In other words, they were primitive pharmacists who were able to provide birth control and abortifacients to their clients.[122]

Saint Paul also condemns this same form of sorcery or *pharmacy*.

> Now the works of the flesh are plain: fornication, impurity, licentiousness, idolatry, sorcery {*pharmakeia*}, enmity, strife, jealousy, anger, selfishness, dissension, party spirit, envy, drunkenness, carousing, and the like. I warn you, as I warned you before, that those who do such things shall not inherit the kingdom of God (Gal 5:19-21).

Surely, Paul does not mean to condemn those who prescribe herbs for those suffering from gout. Looking back to Saint Paul's list, we see that the sin of *pharamakeia* follows sexual sins and the sin of idolatry. These ancient witchdoctors or *pharmacists* were especially popular in idolatrous cultures, since pagan fertility rites often involved sexual orgies. Obviously, the women involved in these depraved rituals would not wish to bear children to strangers, and so they sought to become sterile or sought to relieve themselves of the responsibility of a child through abortion. The ancient Greek *pharmacists* could provide drugs to meet these goals.

The book of Revelation also condemns those who practice *pharmakeia* along with those who practice idolatry, murder, and sexual immorality (Rev 9:20-21). The grouping of *pharmakeia* with the three sins of idolatry, murder, and sexual immorality further confirms that *pharmakeia* is sin relating to killing and sexual impurity. The second-century physician Soranos of Ephesus, in his book *Gynecology*, uses the Greek term *pharmakeia* to refer to potions used for both contraception and abortion. In a similar manner, the third-century theologian Hippolytus condemned certain Christian women who employed "drugs {*pharmakois*} for producing sterility."[123]

Following Saint Paul's condemnation of abortion and *pharmakeia*, the Catholic Church often served as the lone voice in the battle against contraception and abortion. In 1968, Pope Paul VI declared the following:

> We must once again declare that the direct interruption of the generative process already begun, and, above all, directly willed and procured abortion, even if for therapeutic reasons, are to be absolutely excluded as licit means of regulating birth. Equally to be excluded, as the teaching authority of the Church has frequently declared, is direct sterilization, whether perpetual or temporary, whether of the man or of the woman. Similarly excluded is every action which, either in anticipation of the conjugal act, or in its accomplishment, or in the development of its natural consequences, proposes, whether as an end or as a means, to render procreation impossible."[124]

While contraception in itself does not end the life of a living person, it does undermine the intention of the sacrament of marriage whereby the husband and wife make a full act of self-giving in the marital act.

Moreover, Sacred Scripture teaches that children are a blessing.

> Lo, children are a heritage from the LORD, the fruit of the womb a reward. Like arrows in the hand of a warrior are the sons of one's youth.
>
> Happy is the man who has his quiver full of them! He shall not be put to shame when he speaks with his enemies in the gate (Ps 127:3-5).

The Catholic Church has always agreed with the words of this Psalm: "children are a heritage from the Lord. Happy is the man who has a quiver full of them!" We might also recall that Onan was killed by God for spilling his semen outside the womb (cf. Gen 38:9-10). Over and over again, Scripture testifies that fertility is a blessing from the Lord and barrenness is a cause of mourning. To this effect, Saint Paul teaches:

> Yet woman will be saved through bearing children, if she continues in faith and love and holiness, with modesty (1 Tim 2:15).

Granted, this is an obscure passage, but it highlights the esteemed role that women have in bringing new souls into the world. The Christian wife is exhorted to possess "faith and love and holiness, with modesty" but her personal sacrifice of bearing children is esteemed as the greatest response to the grace of God in her life. Just as God the Father is always open to more and more children whom he loves, so also the Catholic parent remains open to this precious gift of life.

The emphasis on the gift of life and the rules and norms for protecting it are essential to Catholic moral teaching. The sexual abuses condemned by the

Apostle Paul can be summed up as an abuse of one of the greatest gifts given to humanity—the ability to cooperate with God's creative power. God could have continued to create human beings just like he created Adam; instead He chose to bring about new persons through the institution of marriage and the family. With this in mind, let us turn to the Catholic concept of a spiritual family. The emphasis on family will help us understand why saints, those whom Paul calls our brothers and sisters, play an important role in Catholic piety and devotion.

NOTES

[112] ἢ οὐκ οἴδατε ὅτι ἄδικοι θεοῦ βασιλείαν οὐ κληρονομήσουσιν; μὴ πλανᾶσθε· οὔτε πόρνοι οὔτε εἰδωλολάτραι οὔτε μοιχοὶ οὔτε μαλακοὶ οὔτε ἀρσενοκοῖται οὔτε κλέπται οὔτε πλεονέκται, οὐ μέθυσοι, οὐ λοίδοροι, οὐχ ἅρπαγες βασιλείαν θεοῦ κληρονομήσουσιν (1 Cor 6:9-10).

[113] The rendering of *koite* as "marriage bed" is attested in both Sophocles and Euripides. The sexual connotation of *koite* is further substantiated by the related negative term ἔχειν κοίτην ἔκ τινος, which can mean, "to be pregnant." See *Liddell & Scott Greek-English Lexicon*, Seventh Edition (Oxford: Oxford University Press, 1997), p. 441.

[114] καὶ ὃς ἂν κοιμηθῇ μετὰ ἄρσενος κοίτην γυναικός, βδέλυγμα ἐποίησαν ἀμφότεροι, θανατούσθωσαν, ἔνοχοί εἰσιν (Lev 20:13 LXX).

[115] Josephus, *Antiquities of the Jews*, 4, 8, 40.

NOTES CONTINUED

[116] Saint Thomas Aquinas, *Summa theologiae* II-II, q. 154, a. 11.

[117] *Catechism of the Catholic Church* §2352.

[118] *Catechism of the Catholic Church* §2357.

[119] *Catechism of the Catholic Church* §2358-9.

[120] Coppens, Charles. "Abortion," *The Catholic Encyclopedia,* Vol. 1. New York: Robert Appleton Company, 1907.

[121] *Didache* 2:2. The Greek word used here for abortion is φθορά.

[122] The most common ancient abortifacient was silphium, grown and exported from Cyrene.

[123] Saint Hippolytus, *The Refutation of All Heresies* 9, 12, 25.

[124] Pope Paul VI, *Humanae Vitae,* 14.

11. Paul on the Communion of the Saints

...surrounded by a great cloud of witnesses...
HEBREWS 12:1

Mystic Sweet Communion

MANY ARE FAMILIAR WITH that beautiful hymn written in 1866 by Samuel John Stone titled "The Church's One Foundation." The final verse reads thus:

> Yet she on earth hath union
> with God, the Three in one,
> and mystic sweet communion
> with those whose rest is won.
> O happy ones and holy!
> Lord, give us grace that we
> like them, the meek and lowly,
> on high may dwell with thee.

Although he was not a Catholic, Samuel John Stone beautifully described the Catholic doctrine of the communion of the saints. There is a certain "mystic sweet communion" experienced by Christians on earth with "those whose rest is won." As Solomon stated, "Love is stronger than death" (Song 8:6). The fellowship that we have with our brothers and sisters in Christ is not broken by death. In fact, our relationship to the saints in heaven is stronger now than it could have been on earth, since those saints are face to face with God and are filled with perfect charity. We remain in communion with the saints in heaven because we remain in union with Christ, who is the Head of the whole body (Col 1:18). Since we are partakers in Christ, we are also partakers in the well being of one another.

There is confusion over what constitutes a "saint." The Greek word literally means "holy one." Saint Paul often uses the term in general for any Christian, since each has received sanctifying grace through baptism, for example: "So then you are no longer strangers and sojourners, but you are fellow citizens with the saints and members of the household of God" (Eph 2:19). However, the word "saint" can also be used in an absolute sense—for those who have actually become fully and completely holy in heaven. We might refer to those already in heaven as "Saints spelled with a capital *S*." Paul contrasts our state with the state of the blessed in heaven in this way:

> For now we see in a mirror dimly, but then face to face. Now I know in part; then I shall understand fully, even as I have been fully understood (1 Cor 13:12).

The saints on earth are united with the saints in heaven, but those in heaven have already attained the fullness of sanctity, whereas we on earth have not. There are also those holy souls who are being cleansed in the state of purgation. The Body of Christ consists of all three groups: those on earth, those in purgatory, and those in heaven.

From the days of the Apostles, Christians understood that they were "surrounded by a great cloud of witnesses" (Heb 12:1), by those departed saints who had gone before them. Early Christian tombs demonstrate that Christians venerated those who had lived and died for the faith as martyrs. They continued to ask for their prayers and prayed for those who had perhaps died less than prepared. In many cases, early Christians celebrated the Eucharist over the tombs of the martyrs.

Despite this early testimony, the Protestant Reformation called into question the Catholic Church's doctrine of the communion of the saints. Martin Luther and those after him appealed to a passage from Saint Paul against the Catholic teaching of the communion of the saints: "For there is one God, and there is one mediator between God and men, the man Christ Jesus" (1 Tim 2:5). This verse was thought to highlight the unique role of Christ in heaven and thereby undermine the Catholic practice of praying to saints in heaven. However, the Protestants made one simple error. The Catholic doctrine teaches that Christians everywhere, both on earth and in heaven, must seek the mediation of Jesus Christ, because He is both fully God and fully man. Yes, Christ is the one mediator between God and man. Christ mediates the prayers of Saint Peter and Saint Paul, and Christ mediates my prayers. The mediating role of Christ does not contradict our willingness to pray for one another, so long as we address our prayers "through Christ our Lord."

If the Catholic woman troubled by infertility seeks the prayers of Saint Elizabeth (a woman who suffered from infertility), then she also assumes that Saint Elizabeth addresses her prayers "through Christ our Lord." Saint Elizabeth and the other saints do not sidestep the mediation of Christ. The saints have the same mediator as we on earth enjoy—the Lord Jesus Christ. Asking for the prayers of saints is similar to asking for a friend on earth to pray for you.

Elsewhere, Saint Paul asks for the prayers of other Christians without any worry that their prayers undermine the sole mediation of Christ.

> Pray at all times in the Spirit, with all prayer and supplication. To that end keep alert with all perseverance, making supplication for all the saints, and also for me (Eph 6:18-20).

Saint Paul also teaches that all Christians should pray for other people:

> First of all, then, I urge that supplications, prayers, intercessions, and thanksgivings be made for all men (1 Tim 2:1).

The Catholic Church believes that Paul's exhortation continues to apply to the saints in heaven. The bond of charity between those in heaven and those on earth leads the heavenly saints to participate in the prayerful mediation of Christ. The saints in heaven pray to Christ for the saints on earth. Even more, if the saints in heaven are full of grace and stand resplendent before the throne of Christ, how much more powerful are their prayers? "The prayer of a righteous man has great power in its effects" (Jas 5:16).

One Body, Many Members

The Catholic Church's doctrine of the communion of the saints is expressed no more clearly than in Saint Paul's First Epistle to the Corinthians. Here, the Apostle describes the Church as the Body of Christ. All Christians participate in Christ's Body and are consequently members of His Body through baptism, as Paul explains:

> For just as the body is one and has many
> members, and all the members of the body,
> though many, are one body, so it is with Christ.
> For by one Spirit we were all baptized into one
> body—Jews or Greeks, slaves or free—and all
> were made to drink of one Spirit. For the body
> does not consist of one member but of many
> (1 Cor 12:12-14).

Paul turns to his sacramental language of participation
to identify how we come to enter into the Body of
Christ: "we were all baptized into one body." This
means that the baptized belong to the Body of Christ
and their physical deaths do not remove them from this
fellowship. Rather, natural death brings Christians more
deeply into the Body of Christ, since they become more
perfectly united with their Head, Jesus Christ.

Every part is therefore necessary for the Body of
Christ to function at its full capacity. We should not
believe that God demotes Christians to a dormant status
when they die. Instead, their function in the Body of
Christ becomes even more powerful as they pray for
those still on earth. Saint Paul explains how one part of
the body cannot be without the other parts:

> The eye cannot say to the hand, "I have no need
> of you," nor again the head to the feet, "I have
> no need of you." On the contrary, the parts of
> the body which seem to be weaker are
> indispensable, and those parts of the body
> which we think less honorable we invest with
> the greater honor, and our unpresentable parts
> are treated with greater modesty, which our
> more presentable parts do not require. But God
> has so composed the body, giving the greater
> honor to the inferior part, that there may be no

> discord in the body, but that the members may
> have the same care for one another (1 Cor
> 12:21-25).

According to Paul, all the members of the Body of
Christ "have the same care for one another." The
Blessed Virgin Mary, therefore, has care for us on earth.
Saint Peter has care for the Church. Saint Paul has care
for us. Every saint in heaven continues to have care for
those on earth and prays for us accordingly.

Veneration of the Saints and Relics

When a soldier salutes his flag, he does not commit the
sin of idolatry. When a child kisses a picture of his
mother, he also does not commit the sin of idolatry.
Everyone accepts a plain distinction between worship
and veneration. As we all know, a courteous bow to the
Queen of England does not amount to idolatry. We can
venerate our founding fathers and even erect
monuments and statues to their memory. We can also
honor them in song and appointed holidays. So likewise,
the Catholic Church shows veneration to the saints of
Jesus Christ—with monuments, statues, artwork, and
feast days.

This principle is based on the words of Saint
Paul: "If one member is honored, all rejoice together.
Now you are the body of Christ and individually
members of it" (1 Cor 12:26-27). If we honor the
Blessed Virgin Mary or Saint Paul, we rejoice together.
In fact, Saint Paul expects us to honor one another. This
honor does not show disrespect for God; instead, such
honor magnifies the glory of God the Father.

If someone pays honor to my son, he pays
honor to me. The same is true of our Heavenly Father
and his beloved children. Nevertheless, the Catholic
Church draws the line between how God is worshiped

and how the saints should be honored. The Seventh Ecumenical Council in Nicea (A.D. 787) decreed that God is given worship or adoration {Greek, *latria*}. The saints on the other hand are given honor or veneration {Greek, *dulia*}. The Catholic Church has never worshiped saints as if they were gods and goddesses. They are human beings, vastly inferior to Christ who is fully God and fully man. Yet, just as there are statues and monuments of George Washington, Thomas Jefferson, and Abraham Lincoln in Washington, D.C., so the Catholic Church erects monuments to the great saints of the Church, traditionally over the bodily remains of the saints. The veneration of relics may seem odd to some, but it corresponds to the Catholic Church's belief in the resurrection of the body at the final Judgment Day. Our bodies will once again be reunited to our souls and raised up to new life. Hence, Catholics show the utmost respect for the bodies of the deceased. Saint Luke records this practice in the earliest days of the Church: "Devout men buried Stephen, and made great lamentation over him" (Acts 8:2). These physical remains or relics were said to effect miracles from time to time. In fact, Saint Augustine testified that even in his day, the relics of Saint Stephen were still procuring miracles of healing to those who sought the prayers of Saint Stephen.[125]

   When non-Catholics observe the Catholic practice of venerating the departed, they often assume that Catholics possess a morbid fascination with death. Against the Catholic Church, many cite Mark 12:26-27, in which Christ proclaims, "God is not the God of the dead, but of the living." Yet this verse affirms the Catholic teaching that the departed saints are not "dead" but "living." When a Catholic asks a saint for prayers, he is not conjuring the dead but speaking to the living, even to one who is more alive than himself—for the saints are fully alive with Christ in heaven.

Even Sacred Scripture attests to the miracles effected by the bones and relics of saints. Elisha's bones brought life to a dead man as soon as the dead man's body came into contact with the relics of the prophet (2 Kgs 13:20-21). We also learn of how the garment of Christ healed a hemorrhaging woman (Mt 9:20-22). Moreover, we find a practice related to relics particularly in the case of Saint Paul:

> And God did extraordinary miracles by the hands of Paul, so that handkerchiefs or aprons were carried away from his body to the sick, and diseases left them and the evil spirits came out of them (Acts 19:11).

These "handkerchiefs and aprons" would be reckoned as "second class relics," since they were not actually body parts of the saint, but rather items brought into contact with Saint Paul's body. Clearly, Saint Paul did not object to this practice, since he allowed it to continue. God chooses to effect miracles through objects that have come into contact with the body of a holy person. These divine miracles attest to Saint Paul's words: "If one member is honored, all rejoice together. Now you are the body of Christ and individually members of it" (1 Cor 12:26-27). We find in the Catholic Church's doctrine of saints and miracles the Pauline emphasis on participation.

We also find an emphasis on the incarnation of Christ and the extended manifestation of His body in the bodies of His saints. Saints, relics, and other religious objects go hand in hand with the Church's sacramental belief that God accomplishes salvation and miracles through physical means. To expand on our theme of participation, the relics of the saints participate in the redemptive power of Christ.

What about the Virgin Mary?

Catholics have a profound love and devotion for the Blessed Virgin Mary as the Mother of their Savior. This devotion is deeply incarnational, since Mary was the chosen vessel by which the divine "Word became flesh and dwelt among us" (Jn 1:14). Christ offered His flesh and blood on the cross for our salvation—the flesh and blood that He acquired from his earthly mother. Since Saint Paul's theology is centered on the incarnation of Christ and our participation in Him as "the body of Christ," we might expect that Paul had much to say about the Virgin Mother of Christ. Yet Saint Paul mentions the Blessed Virgin Mary only once in his epistles, and there rather briefly:

> But when the fullness of time had come, God sent forth his Son, born of *woman*, born under the law, to redeem those who were under the law, so that we might receive adoption as sons. And because you are sons, God has sent the Spirit of his Son into our hearts, crying, "Abba! Father!" (Gal 4:4-6).

Paul does not even mention her name. Saint Paul mentions neither her virginity nor the miraculous birth of Christ. The Catholic looks in vain for Paul's description of Mary as immaculately conceived or as assumed into heaven. One might conclude, then, that Saint Paul's theology and mysticism is Christocentric in a way that excludes Marian devotion.

On the contrary, there is an obvious reason for Paul's lack of attention to the Blessed Virgin Mary. Saint Paul concerned himself with those doctrines that were challenged by emerging heretics. Saint Paul burdened his pen with two doctrinal issues in particular: 1) the doctrine that baptized Christians are free from the Law of Moses and circumcision; and 2) the doctrine of Christ's bodily resurrection. The absence of the Virgin Mary's name from the writings of Paul should not be understood as a slight against her. In fact, Paul's description of Christ's mother as the "woman" in Galatians 4:4-6 is perhaps *the* most profound passage about the Blessed Virgin Mary in the entire New Testament. We might even argue that Paul's description of "the woman" is even more profound than Saint Luke's description of Mary as "full of grace" (Lk 1:28), as "mother of the Lord" (Lk 1:43), or as Saint John's apocalyptic description of the "woman clothed with the sun with the moon under her feet" (Rev 11:19-12:17).[126]

The Catholic Church also discovers Paul's rich contribution to Mariology in this brief passage, which is worth citing once more:

> But when the fullness of time had come, God sent forth his Son, born of *woman*, born under the law, to redeem those who were under the law, so that we might receive adoption as sons. And because you are sons, God has sent the Spirit of his Son into our hearts, crying, "Abba! Father!" (Gal 4:4-6)

Paul's reference to Mary as the "woman" is as hard on our ears in English as it is in Greek. To refer to anyone's mother simply as *that woman* seems somewhat odd and offensive. However, Paul's use of "woman" reveals that he is already keenly aware of the role of the Mother of the Messiah as the "Woman" foretold in Genesis 3:15:

> I will put enmity between you [Satan] and the
> woman, and between your seed and her seed.
> He shall bruise your head, and you shall bruise
> his heel (Gen 3:15).

This passage, known as the *Protoevangelium* or "First
Gospel," is the divine promise to Adam and Eve that a
"woman" will one day give birth to a "seed" that will
crush Satan's head. In brief, this is the first divine
promise of redemption—the first Gospel message.

Adam and Eve were saved by believing in this
promise from God. They did not know the details of
the Apostles' Creed. Nevertheless, they hoped in the
coming of a Redeemer—born of woman—who would
defeat the serpent that beguiled them into sin and death.
The title preferred by Jesus Christ and the Apostles for
the Blessed Virgin Mary is simply "woman," since it
captures the exact wording of the *Protoevangelium* in
Genesis 3:15. She is almost exclusively called "woman"
throughout the New Testament:

✠ And Jesus said to her, "O *Woman*, what have
you to do with me? My hour has not yet come"
(Jn 2:4).

✠ When Jesus saw his mother, and the disciple
whom he loved standing near, he said to his
mother, "*Woman* behold your son!" (Jn 19:26).

✠ But when the time had fully come, God sent
forth his Son, born of *woman* (Gal 4:4).

✠ And a great portent appeared in heaven, a *woman*
clothed with the sun, with the moon under her
feet, and on her head a crown of twelve stars
(Rev 12:1).

✠ His tail swept down a third of the stars of
heaven, and cast them to the earth. And the
dragon stood before the *woman* who was about

to bear a child, that he might devour her child when she brought it forth (Rev 12:4).

✠ The *woman* fled into the wilderness, where she has a place prepared by God, in which to be nourished for one thousand two hundred and sixty days (Rev 12:6).

✠ When the dragon saw that he had been thrown down to the earth, he pursued the *woman* who had borne the male Child (Rev 12:13).

✠ Then the dragon was angry with the *woman*, and went off to make war on the rest of her offspring, on those who keep the commandments of God and bear testimony of Jesus (Rev 12:17).

Notably, Mary is called the *woman* at key moments in the New Testament, that is, when Christ worked His first miracle at Cana by changing water into wine ("O *Woman*, what have you to do with me?"), when Christ hangs upon the cross for human redemption ("Woman behold your son!"), and finally in the apocalypse when the ancient battle between Eve and the Serpent is reenacted with Mary as the "woman" who gives birth to Christ, thereby conquering the draconian Satan in fulfillment of God's promise in Genesis 3:15.

So then, Paul's use of "woman" and "the fullness of time" refers back to the ancient promise of God that a "woman" would give birth to a Son that would conquer Satan "in the fullness of time." Ruggero Rossini explains how Paul draws out four profound lessons in these three brief verses from Galatians, namely:

1. The predestination of Christ as the goal of creation.

2. The predestination of Christ realized *in time*.
3. Mary's divine and spiritual motherhood.
4. Our adoption as children of God.[127]

Christ's birth "when the fullness of time had come" refers to the divine plan to reestablish all things in Christ, as Paul states in Ephesians:

> For he has made known to us in all wisdom and insight the mystery of his will, according to his purpose which he set forth in Christ *a plan for the fullness of time* to unite all things in him, things in heaven and things on earth (Eph 1:9-10).

In Galatians 4:4-6, Paul shows how redemption centers on Christ being "born of a woman, born under the law that He might redeem those who were under the Law." Mary is the transition from Law to Grace, since Christ, who was above the Law, came to be born under the Law through her womb. She is daughter of Zion—the embodiment of true Israel and the first believer in the Incarnate Messiah.

As early as the seventh century, the bishop and martyr Saint Andrew of Crete († A.D. 712) recognized the importance of this truth. From Saint Paul's teaching that our adoption as sons depended on Christ's "being born of a woman," Saint Andrew of Crete preached that Mary was therefore the "Mediatrix of Law and Grace,"[128] since her womb became the place where the divine Son of God became a slave to the Law so that we sinners might become adopted sons through the Son. Our adoption as sons of God the Father occurs through this interchange at the incarnation. God becomes our Father so that we can say "Abba! Father!" Yet Mary also becomes our mother since we are co-heirs with Christ.

Everything Christ has we also inherit—this includes His mother. This is why Christ says from the cross, "Woman behold your son." The book of Revelation also teaches that Christians are the children of Mary: "Then the dragon was angry with *the woman*, and went off to make war *on the rest of her offspring, on those who keep the commandments of God and bear testimony to Jesus*" (Jn 20:17). If we stand at the foot of the cross, Jesus says, "Behold thy mother." If we bear the testimony of Jesus, then we are "the rest of her offspring."

Saint Paul's Mariology might seem scarce; however, we learn from Paul that Mary's motherhood is linked to our adoption in Christ. As Rossini observed, this Pauline text in Galatians "contains within itself a good part of Mariology, if not the whole of Mariology."[129] Moreover, our Pauline study of Mary does not end with Galatians. In fact, Paul's closest disciple provides us with wonderfully vivid accounts of the Mother of Christ. We refer, of course, to Saint Luke the Evangelist.

In Saint Luke's Gospel and the Acts of the Apostles, we find an intimate account of the Blessed Virgin Mary. Tradition states that Luke gained his information about Mary directly from the Blessed Virgin herself, when Paul and Luke returned to Jerusalem sometime around the year A.D. 58. Tradition also holds that Saint Luke painted a portrait of the Blessed Virgin Mary on the wooden tabletop that had belonged to the Holy Family. Whether or not this legend is true, the portrait of the Blessed Virgin Mary as presented in the Gospel of Luke and Acts is quite stunning.

Saint Luke begins by recording the miraculous meeting of the angel Gabriel with the young Virgin Mary:

> The angel Gabriel was sent from God to a city
> of Galilee named Nazareth, to a virgin betrothed
> to a man whose name was Joseph, of the house
> of David; and the virgin's name was Mary. And
> he came to her and said, "Hail, full of grace, the
> Lord is with you!" (Lk 1:26-28).

The remarkable feature of this account is the angel's greeting to the young virgin. Saint Gabriel cries out "Hail, full of grace, the Lord is with you!" This was not a common greeting in antiquity, and so Mary "considered in her mind what sort of greeting this might be" (Lk 1:29). Saint Luke renders "full of grace" by the Greek word *kecharitomene*. It is the perfect passive participle of the verb meaning "to grace." The perfect tense denoting a past action—the action has already come to completion. Since it is passive, we see that something has happened to the person described, that is, something has happened to the Blessed Virgin Mary. Thus, we may even translate the angel's greeting as "Hail, she who has been perfectly graced" or more simply "Hail, full of grace."

Citing the title "full of grace," Pope Pius IX proclaimed in 1854:

> The most Blessed Virgin Mary was, from the
> first moment of her conception, by a singular
> grace and privilege of almighty God and by
> virtue of the merits of Jesus Christ, Savior of the
> human race, preserved immune from all stain of
> original sin.[130]

Similarly, the Eastern Fathers call the Blessed Virgin Mary "the All-Holy" {*Panagia*}, and celebrate her as free from any stain of sin:: "Thou and thy mother are the only ones who are totally beautiful in every respect; for in thee, O Lord, there is not spot, and in they mother no stain."[131]

Saint Luke's praiseworthy account of the Blessed Virgin Mary does not cease here. After the departure of the angel Gabriel, Mary visited her relative Elizabeth who was pregnant with the baby who would be named John the Baptist. The Blessed Mother arrived at the house of Elizabeth and greeted her:

> And when Elizabeth heard the greeting of Mary, the babe leaped in her womb—and Elizabeth was filled with the Holy Spirit and she exclaimed with a loud cry, "*Blessed are you among women*, and blessed is the fruit of your womb! And why is this granted me, that the *mother of my Lord* should come to me? (Lk 1:41-43)

According to Elizabeth, Mary is "blessed among women," because she is the "mother of the Lord." Furthermore, Luke also records Mary's own words in this regard: "All generations will call me blessed" (Lk 1:48). Catholics therefore affix "Blessed" to her name and titles. Moreover, Catholics pray the Holy Rosary as a devotional exercise seeking to fulfill her prophecy that all generations will call her "blessed."

Saint Elizabeth also calls the Blessed Virgin Mary "the mother of my Lord" (Lk 1:43). For this reason, the Catholic Church also invokes the Blessed Mother by the title *Theotokos,* Greek for or "Mother of God." Saint Ignatius of Antioch who was martyred around A.D. 108 wrote, "For our God Jesus Christ was carried in Mary's womb according to God's resolve of salvation."[132] Scholars have found references to the Mary being called *Theotokos* as early as the second or third century. Origen, Saint Alexander of Alexandria, and Saint Athanasius used the title for the Blessed Virgin.

Catholic tradition also finds in the Gospel of Luke a description of Mary as the "Ark of the Covenant." Elizabeth's acclamation, "Why is this granted me, that the mother of my Lord should come to me?" parallels a comment made by David, "How is it that the ark of the Lord should come to me?" (2 Sam 6:9). Moreover, the Ark of Covenant remained in the hill country of Judea "for three months" (2 Sam 6:11). Likewise, Mary also remained in the hill country of Judea "for three months" (Lk 1:56). Lastly, David leapt before the Ark of the Covenant, and the baby in Elizabeth's womb also "leapt" in the presence of the pregnant Virgin Mary (Lk 1:41). These three literary parallels have led the Catholic Church to see the Blessed Virgin Mary as the Ark of the *New* Covenant, because she bears within herself the body and blood of the New Covenant, whereas the Ark of the Old Covenant contained the stone tablets of the Law. When we consider the sanctity of the Ark of the Covenant, we come to appreciate the sanctity of the Blessed Virgin Mary.

Saint Luke also records for us that the Blessed Virgin Mary was present on the great day of Pentecost.

> All these with one accord devoted themselves to prayer, together with the women and *Mary the mother of Jesus*, and with his brothers. In those days Peter stood up among the brethren—the company of persons was in all about a hundred and twenty (Acts 1:12-15).

Saint Luke preserves Saint Paul's doctrine of participation with respect to the Body of Christ by structuring his Gospel and the Acts of the Apostles in a similar fashion. Mary stands at the beginning of the Gospel of Luke in the account of the birth of Christ, and also at the beginning of the Acts of the Apostles when the Church was born on the day of Pentecost. By highlighting this arrangement, we observe that Mary is the mother of the Christ and the mother of the Church. Mary is the Mother of the Head and the Mother of the Body. The two are inseparable. "Christ is the head of the Church, His body, and is Himself its Savior" (Eph 5:23). The incarnation of Christ through the Blessed Virgin Mary enables all Christians to participate in Christ—not only in His life, but also in His death. In the next chapter, we will explore how Saint Paul literally fulfilled this mystery by suffering constantly with Christ—even unto death as a witness to Christ's crucified love for all men.

NOTES

[125] Saint Augustine, *City of God* 22, 8.

[126] Incidentally, Plato and Aristotle held that the region below the moon was the realm of change while the region above the moon was unchanging. For the ancients, then, the moon was the boundary between this world below and the world above. Saint John's apocalyptic vision of the Mother of Christ *above* the moon signifies that she is no longer of this temporal realm—she has been assumed body and soul into heaven.

[127] Ruggero Rossini, *The Mariology of John Duns Scotus*, Translated by Peter M. Fehlner (New Bedford, MA: Academy of the Immaculate, 2008), 1-2.

[128] Saint Andrew of Crete, *Sermon on the Nativity of the Blessed Virgin Mary* PG 97, 865a. The Armenian

NOTES CONTINUED

Liturgy likewise invokes Mary as the "Mediatrix of Law and Grace. See V. Tekeyan, "La Mère de Dieu dans la liturgie armenienne," in *Maria. Etudes surla Sainte Vierge*, ed. H. du Manoir, S.J., v. 1, Paris, 1949, p. 359.

[129] Rossini, 6.

[130] Pius IX, *Ineffabilis Deus* (1854). Denzinger-Schonmetzer, *Enchridion Symbolorum* (1965), 2803.

[131] Saint Ephrem the Syrian, *Carm. Nisib. 27.*

[132] Saint Ignatius of Antioch, *Eph 18, 2.*

12. THE MARTYRDOM & DEATH OF PAUL

…I have been crucified with Christ…
GALATIANS 2:20

…I complete what is lacking in Christ's afflictions
for the sake of His body, that is, the Church…
COLOSSIANS 1:24

The Problem of Pain

NEARLY EVERY RELIGION SEEKS to make sense of the problem of pain. If God is both omnibenificent {all-loving} and omnipotent {all-powerful}, why then does He allow us to suffer? The Eastern traditions such as Buddhism dismiss pain and suffering as "unreal." This solution is difficult to explain to a child with cancer. Other religious traditions attempt to accrue "good karma" in order to ensure that good times will come with a future reincarnated life. For these traditions, the origin of suffering is past sins, even sins committed in previous lives. Still other religions, such as Islam, seem to place the origin of suffering in the capricious "will of Allah."

Knowing Christ Crucified

The Catholic Faith offers an entirely different account of suffering, because the Church holds up the crucified Christ as the archetype for Christian living. No doubt, the Church is obsessed with the crucifix, and that for good reason. The crucified Christ provides the meaning of life and the meaning of death, even the meaning of the life to come! The suffering of Christ does not prevent our suffering on earth, but it does allow us to suffer with dignity and meaning. Saint Paul indicates that every authentic Christian will suffer in this world:

> For it has been granted to you that for the sake of Christ you should not only believe in him but also suffer for his sake (Phil 1:29).

It was for this reason that the Apostle Paul focused the attention of his spiritual life on the crucifixion of Christ:

> For I decided to know nothing among you except Jesus Christ and Him crucified (1 Cor 2:2).

This "crucifixion mentality" is one that Paul sought to instill in his disciples. When the Apostle perceived heresy in the Church in Galatia, he realized that they had forgotten their identity as followers of the crucified Christ:

> Who has bewitched you, before whose eyes Jesus Christ was publicly portrayed as crucified? (Gal 3:1)

The glib Protestant adage, "But we worship the resurrected Christ, not the crucified Christ" finds no traction in the writings of Paul. One cannot divide Christ. There is not a "resurrected Jesus" and a "crucified Jesus." There is one Lord Jesus Christ and His resurrection possesses meaning for us only in so far as we appreciate His crucifixion. Moreover, Saint Paul indicates that if we wish to attain the resurrected glory of Christ we must first enter into the sufferings of His death:

> That I may know him and the power of His resurrection, and may share His sufferings, becoming like Him in his death, that if possible I may attain the resurrection from the dead (Phil 3:10-11).

Paul also states that we are "fellow heirs with Christ, provided that we suffer with Him" (Rom 8:17). Moreover, Saint Luke also preserved the words of Christ to this effect: "Whoever does not bear his own cross and come after me, cannot be my disciple" (Lk 14:27).

A person will carry the cross only if the cross carries meaning. The cross swallows every sin and every pain. When Adam and Eve sinned, they brought mankind into the state of original sin, as we observed in an earlier chapter. "Therefore as sin came into the world through one man and death through sin, and so death spread to all men" (Rom 5:12). God permits the suffering of mankind on account of sin. Yet, God did not choose to remain outside of our sufferings. Instead, He entered into our sufferings. Jesus Christ experienced the hardships of humanity. He experienced poverty, hunger, thirst, false accusations, persecutions, and even a bloody death. Christ our Lord has experienced pain and death, and so when we unite our own sufferings to those of Christ, our personal sufferings take on redemptive power. Saint Paul explains how through Christ he transformed physical hardships into spiritual strength:

> I will all the more gladly boast of my
> weaknesses, that the power of Christ may rest
> upon me. For the sake of Christ, then, I am
> content with weaknesses, insults, hardships,
> persecutions, and calamities. For when I am
> weak, then I am strong (2 Cor 12:9-10).

Many well-meaning Christians are repulsed by the
crucifix, because it displays the weakness of Christ.
However, the cross teaches us that Christ transformed
His greatest moment of physical weakness into the most
potent act of redemptive suffering. Christ's death is our
salvation. The Catholic Church guards as a precious
jewel the paradox that states, "when I am weak, then I
am strong," or alternatively: "death brings forth life."
Because of this, Saint Paul perceived his own vocation
as a ministry of redemptive suffering:

> We are afflicted in every way, but not crushed;
> perplexed, but not driven to despair; persecuted,
> but not forsaken; struck down, but not
> destroyed; always carrying in the body the death
> of Jesus, so that the life of Jesus may also be
> manifested in our bodies. For while we live we
> are always being given up to death for Jesus'
> sake, so that the life of Jesus may be manifested
> in our mortal flesh (2 Cor 4:8-11).

Saint Paul explains that he always carries in his body
"the death of Jesus." When Paul is crushed, persecuted,
struck down, he remains mindful that he bears within
himself the "death of Jesus." The union between Paul's
sufferings and Christ's sufferings results in the
manifestation of Christ's life in the person of Paul.

Saint Paul articulates his doctrine of redemptive suffering in a shocking statement to the Christians in Colossae:

> Now I rejoice in my sufferings for your sake, and *in my flesh I complete what is lacking in Christ's afflictions* for the sake of His body, that is, the Church (Col 1:24).

On the surface, it seems that Saint Paul is uttering blasphemy. How can Paul complete what is *lacking in Christ's afflictions*? Can we possibly speak of there being any lack in the sufferings of Christ? We know that Paul did not wish to diminish the sufferings of Christ, or else he would not have said:

> But far be it from me to glory except in the cross of our Lord Jesus Christ, by which the world has been crucified to me, and I to the world (Gal 6:14).

We might best understand what Paul means by "that which is lacking in Christ's afflictions" as those sufferings that we must experience in this life. Christ's sufferings are complete and efficacious in their own right. We can add nothing to the redemptive suffering of Christ. However, we can unite our sufferings to Christ. This is the element that is "lacking." When we offer our sufferings to Christ, Christ makes them His own in a mysterious way. To this end, Saint Paul even speaks of himself as nailed upon the cross with Christ:

> I have been crucified with Christ. It is no longer I who live, but Christ who lives in me; and the life I now live in the flesh I live by faith in the

> Son of God, who loved me and gave himself for
> me (Gal 2:20).

Ultimately, this is where Saint Paul's doctrine of participation reaches its highest expression. At this point, our book turns full circle. We began with Saint Paul's miraculous experience on the Road to Damascus where he heard those significant words of Christ in Acts 9:4: "Saul, Saul, why do you persecute me?" Unbeknownst to Paul, Saint Stephen and the other persecuted Christians had united their sufferings to the sufferings of Christ. One might even place the words of Paul in the heart of Stephen as he died a martyr's death: "I rejoice in my sufferings for your sake...for the sake of Saul." Perhaps it was the prayerful suffering of Stephen, in union with Christ, that initiated the grace of God toward Saul who stood by holding the coats of those who cast their stones at Stephen, the Church's first martyr.

Saint Paul's Martyrdom in Rome

We have observed that Saint Paul believed the Church to be one, holy, catholic, and apostolic. However, few have recognized that Saint Paul perceived that the Church must also be *Roman*. We have discussed at length the famous conversion of Paul on the road to Damascus when Christ appeared to him surrounded in glorious light. We are less familiar with another apparition of Christ that Paul received after his arrest in Jerusalem in the Spring of A.D. 58.

> The following night the Lord stood by Paul and said, "Take courage, for as you have testified about me at Jerusalem, so you must bear witness also at Rome" (Acts 23:11).

This passage is remarkable because it reveals to us that Jesus Christ Himself ordered Paul to go to Rome. It was a divine appointment. Nowhere else does Christ appear and say, "Go to Athens. Go to Corinth. Go to Ephesus." When Christ speaks again to Paul it is to provide him with an important set of instructions: "You must bear witness also at Rome!"

Paul must also have had an intuition about the goal of his ministry because we find in an earlier passage that Paul is aware of his need to travel to Rome:

> Now after these events Paul resolved in the Spirit to pass through Macedonia and Achaia and go to Jerusalem, saying, "After I have been there, I must also see Rome" (Acts 19:21).

In fact, Luke's Acts of the Apostles is likely a justification for how the Church began in Jerusalem and at lest settled in Rome. One can observe a sense of relief when, in the last chapter of the Acts of the Apostles, Saint Luke writes: "And so we came to Rome" (Acts 28:14). The book abruptly ends with Saint Paul and Luke in the city of Rome with Paul under house arrest. Although Paul was under house arrest, Luke records for us that Paul "welcomed all who came to him, preaching the kingdom of God and teaching about the Lord Jesus Christ quite openly and unhindered" (Acts 28:31). With those words, the Acts of the Apostles comes to a close.

Sacred tradition indicates that Paul was eventually acquitted and embarked on yet another missionary journey. Some rumor him to have visited Spain. He kept Luke with him always. It would seem that Paul visited Crete, and left Titus there as bishop. Paul also left Timothy as bishop in Ephesus. We find Paul again in the city of Rome around the year A.D. 67. Tradition places him there alongside Peter, the Church's first pope. Some accounts say that they received martyrdom on the same day. Peter was crucified (upside down) because he was not a Roman citizen. Saint Paul was a Roman citizen, so he received the honor of being beheaded outside the walls of Rome. Before meeting his death, Paul wrote these words concerning his impending death:

> For I am already on the point of *being sacrificed*. The time of my departure has come. I have fought the good fight, I have finished the race, I have kept the faith. Henceforth there is laid up for me the crown of righteousness, which the Lord, the righteous judge, will award to me on that Day, and not only to me but also to all who have loved his appearing (2 Tim 4:6-8).

Paul's belief that he "carried in his body the death of Jesus" (2 Cor 4:10) led to the sacrifice of his own body. Thirty years previously, Saint Paul had approved of the death of Saint Stephen, the Church's first martyr. Eventually Paul would join that same army of martyrs. He would "offer his body as a living sacrifice, holy and acceptable to God" (Rom 12:1).

We do not possess an official account of his martyrdom, but we do possess the apocryphal *Acts of Saint Paul*, which record the martyrdom of the Apostle in this way:

> Then Paul stood with his face to the east and lifted up his hands unto heaven and prayed a long time. In his prayer he conversed in the Hebrew tongue with the fathers, and then stretched forth his neck without speaking. And when the executioner struck off his head, milk spurted upon the cloak of the soldier. And the

soldier and all that were there present when they saw it marveled and glorified God who had given such glory unto Paul. And they went and told Caesar what was done (*Acts of Paul* 10, 5).

As Paul prayed in the Hebrew language in those last moments before his death, perhaps he lisped a prayer stating what he had previously promised to the Christians in Rome:

> I consider that the sufferings of this present time are not worth comparing with the glory that is to be revealed to us (Rom 8:18).

He had once heard Christ say to him: "Saul, Saul, why do you persecute me?" Now the same man was able to respond, "Lord, Lord, now I am persecuted with thee."

Did you benefit from this book?
Please visit amazon.com and leave a review for this book.
Thank you so much! - Taylor

EPILOGUE:
THE CATHOLIC PAUL WITHIN A TRILOGY

PAUL'S MARTYRDOM IN ROME ends our "Catholic Perspective on Saint Paul," but it also leads us to the threshold of the third and final book of *The Origins of Catholic Christianity* trilogy.

The first book, *The Crucified Rabbi: Judaism and the Origins of Catholic Christianity*, traced the Jewish origins of the teachings and practices of the Catholic Church. It was a book about the Old Testament and its fulfillment in Christ and the Catholic Church.

This second book, *The Catholic Perspective on Paul: Paul and the Origins of Catholic Christianity*, sought to demonstrate that the faith of the Apostles was in fact the Catholic Faith as practiced today. Paul was not a liberal, a heretic, a Protestant, or a gnostic. He was the great Catholic Apostle.

The third book, *The Eternal City: Rome and the Origins of Catholic Christianity*, seeks to do something much more ambitious. It seeks to show that the Old Testament prophesied that the Messianic Kingdom of God would conquer and possess the Roman Empire—that Christ from eternity past had destined His Church to be *Roman*. Our Church is not the Roman Catholic Church by accident. Of course, the martyrdom of Paul plays into this argument, as does a number of other facts. If you enjoyed this book, please look forward to

The Eternal City as we survey the Old Testament prophecies regarding the Roman Empire, the Maccabean alliance with Rome, the particulars of the Incarnation and Crucifixion of the Messiah in their Roman contexts, the significance of Peter as the Pope of Rome, and the eventual conversion of the Roman Empire under Constantine. It's an exciting story. I can't wait to tell it…

Godspeed,
Taylor R. Marshall

APPENDIX 1:
10 CATHOLIC QUESTIONS FOR N.T. WRIGHT

I N THE LAST DECADE, no theologian has been more influential in the realm of Paul scholarship than the Anglican scholar and bishop Nicholas Thomas Wright. Wright received his D.Phil. in 1981 from Merton College, Oxford, with a thesis titled, "The Messiah and the People of God: A Study in Pauline Theology with Particular Reference to the Argument of the Epistle to the Romans." He also stirred the waters of Pauline scholarship with his short book: *What Saint Paul Really Said: Was Paul of Tarsus the Real Founder of Christianity?* (1997). Subsequently, he was appointed as the Anglican Bishop of Durham in 2003 and retired from his office in August of 2010. In recent years, Wright has received criticism for his reevaluation of Martin Luther's presentation of Saint Paul. Reformed Protestants in particular have accused N.T. Wright of moving toward Catholicism on key doctrines, thereby eroding the Protestant doctrine of justification.

As a Reformed and Anglican seminarian, I read Wright thoroughly and I have often stated publicly that Wright's work assisted me along the path to Catholicism. My study of Wright's books and my subsequent conversion to Catholicism was recently noted in an article from *Christianity Today* titled, "Not All Evangelicals and Catholics Together." In this article I wrote the following words:

"If you buy into Wright's approach to covenantal theology, then you've already taken three steps toward the Catholic Church. Keep following the trail and you'll be Catholic," said Marshall.

"Salvation is sacramental, transformational, communal, and eschatological. Sound good? You've just assented to the Catholic Council of Trent."

N.T. Wright responded to my claims in the same article with these words:

"I am sorry to think that there are people out there whose Protestantism has been so barren that they never found out about sacraments, transformation, community, or eschatology. Clearly this person [i.e. Taylor] needed a change. But to jump to Rome for that reason is very odd," he said. "The best Reformed, charismatic, Anglican, and even some emerging churches have these emphases," he said.

N.T. Wright's full response to my comments were later published by Trevin Wax. After reading Wright's full response, I was struck by two seemingly contradictory positions in his writings. On one hand, it seems that Dr. Wright is perhaps less opposed to Catholicism than I had supposed. On the other hand, it seems that he has objections to the Catholic faith that are unwarranted—at least from my point of view.

After pondering this state of affairs, I drafted "Ten Questions" for N.T. Wright regarding Catholicism, justification, and a variety of other topics that he addressed regarding Catholicism. I offer these questions in a spirit of charity and humility—hoping that he might clarify his positions and assist all of us who have read his books with care and admiration.

Ten Questions for N.T. Wright Regarding Catholicism

1. N.T. Wright, in your new book *Justification: God's Plan and Paul's Vision* (page 141) you write concerning 2 Corinthians 5:21:

> The little word *genometha* in 5:21b—'that we might become God's righteousness in him'—does not sit comfortably with the normal interpretation, according to which 'God's righteousness' is 'imputed' or 'reckoned' to believers. If that is what Paul meant, with the overtones of 'extraneous righteousness' that normally come with that theory, the one thing that he ought not to have said is that we 'become' that righteousness. Surely that leans far too much towards a Roman Catholic notion of infused righteousness? How careless of Paul to leave the door open to such a notion!

FIRST QUESTION: You seem to indicate here that Saint Paul does in fact teach the "Roman Catholic notion of infused righteousness." How would we be wrong if we were to assume that you are here denying justification by imputation and favoring "a Roman Catholic notion of infused righteousness"?

2. Also in *Justification: God's Plan and Paul's Vision* (p. 164), you wrote: "what damage to genuine pastoral theology has been done by making a bogey-word out of the Pauline term *synergism*, "working together with God."

SECOND QUESTION: Should we conclude that you agree with the Council of Trent regarding synergism and disagree with Luther and Calvin on monergism?

3. Dr. Wright, on p. 230, you write:

> Thus when [John] Piper says (22) that "Wright makes startling statements to the effect that our future justification will be on the basis of works," I want to protest: it isn't Wright who says this, but Paul.

Your words conform nicely to the Council of Trent's Session Six, Chapter 10: "faith co-operating with good works, increase in that justice which they have received through the grace of Christ, and are still further justified."

THIRD QUESTION: Are you not affirming with Session Six of the Council of Trent that our justification (with it's future implications) will be on the basis of works? John Piper doesn't want to let you off the hook on this one.

4. Dr. Wright, in *What Saint Paul Really Said* (page 119) you wrote that justification is about ecclesiology before soteriology. This lines up nicely with Session Six of the Council of Trent (especially Chapter Seven), which relates justification in the traditional terms of catechumens and the Church.

FOURTH QUESTION: How is your teaching in *What Saint Paul Really Said* substantially different from the Council of Trent's formulation?

QUESTIONS FOR N.T. WRIGHT

5. Dr. Wright, you note that Heinrich Schlier was a fine New Testament scholar. On the other hand, you wrote that Heinrich Schlier, "found that the only way to be a Protestant was to be a Bultmannian, so, because he couldn't take Bultmann, he became a Roman Catholic; that was the only other option in his culture." Yet, Schlier states that it was Sacred Scripture that lead him into the Catholic Church.

FIFTH QUESTION: Do you believe that the brilliant Heinrich Schlier believed that being Bultmannian or being Catholic were the *only* two options available to him? Could not have Scripture converted him to the Catholic faith?

6. Dr. Wright, you state that the Council of Trent provided the wrong answer regarding "nature/grace question." As far as I can tell, Trent only touched upon this question in Session Five, and even there the word "nature" only appears twice.

SIXTH QUESTION: Could you clarify what you mean by "Trent gave the wrong answer, at a deep level, to the nature/grace question"? To which session would I turn in the Council of Trent to find the alleged "wrong answer"?

7. Dr. Wright, you state that Trent's "wrong answer to the nature/grace question" led to Catholic abuses in Marian doctrine and devotion.

SEVENTH QUESTION: Are you referring to something as general as the prayers to Mary or something more specific like her bodily assumption into heaven?

8. You indicated that the Catholic Church has sought to prevent the belief that God works through women and lay people. You summarize the Catholic position as:

> Communal, yes, but don't let the laity (or the women) get any fancy ideas about God working new things through them.

Dr. Wright, surely you do not believe the Catholic Church thinks this way. It is rather noteworthy that the two greatest saints of the Catholic Church are the Blessed Virgin Mary (a woman) and Saint Joseph (a layman).

Our profound love for the Blessed Virgin Mary and her role in the incarnation goes without mentioning. Moreover, the Catholic Church venerates three female Doctors of the Church (St Teresa of Avila, St Catherine of Sienna, and St Therese of Lisieux) who stand next to the other great Doctors of the Church like St Augustine, St Basil, St Thomas Aquinas, et al.

EIGHTH QUESTION: Could you be more specific as to how the Catholic Church devalues the role of women and laymen?

9. You write that the Reformed, Anglican, charismatic, and emergent traditions can encompass the best of what it means to be what I call, "sacramental, transformational, communal, eschatological." Yet, these four traditions (Reformed, Anglican, Charismatic, and Emergent) are in fundamental disagreement over what a sacrament is, how a human is justified and/or sanctified, what the Church is, and what the eschaton is and how it will occur. Even within their own jurisdictions (take the Anglican Communion for example), there is vast

disagreement over each of these issues. You say there are "bits of it" in the emergent church, but we could also say that there are "bits of it" whenever we pray the Our Father, yet "bits of it" do not entail the climax of the covenant as anticipated in Isaiah, Daniel, or the Minor Prophets, and as you indicated in your books.

NINTH QUESTION: If what it means to be sacramental, transformational, communal, eschatological "can be found in" these four contradicting traditions, doesn't it entail that each of these four (or even all four together) do not actualize what it means to be sacramental, transformational, communal, eschatological? In other words, "these elements can be found in their congregations" does not entail "these elements constitute their congregations."

10. Dr. Wright, you write:

> Trent, and much subsequent RC theology, has had a habit of never spring-cleaning, so you just live in a house with more and more clutter building up, lots of right answers to wrong questions.

Yet isn't it the case that since the Reformation, only the Catholic Church has continued to hold councils and examine the deposit of faith? Lutherans, Anglicans, and Calvinists still appeal to the same dusty articles of faith that they drafted in the sixteenth and seventeenth centuries. They do not hold doctrinal councils. They are unable to reform. They are what they are. So the accusation that the Catholic Church does not clean house is actually more appropriately directed toward Protestant denominations, including the Anglican Communion.

TENTH QUESTION: Is it the case that Protestant theology is clean and tidy when compared to Catholic theology?

Dr. Wright, you wrote concerning me:

> I am sorry to think that there are people out there whose Protestantism has been so barren that they never found out about sacraments, transformation, community or eschatology. Clearly this person [i.e. Taylor] needed a change. But to jump to Rome for that reason is very odd.

Please know that I am not simply an isolated "this person" who "needed a change." I'm not the only one. Thousands and thousands of clergy and laity from your own denomination have appealed to the Pope as a result of the Anglican Communion losing its sacramental and communal nature. If Anglicanism can provide a form of Christianity that is "sacramental, transformational, communal, and eschatological," then why are these Anglicans so deeply dissatisfied with Anglicanism? Why also are there scores of former Protestants who are now Catholic *and attribute their conversion, in part, to reading N.T. Wright's books?* Dr. Wright, would you also say that their "jump to Rome" is "very odd"?

As a grateful fan and reader of N.T. Wright's books, I am continually amazed by his profound insights into Sacred Scripture. As a Catholic, I continue to enjoy his books and find myself returning to his works on a regular basis. I have the highest regard for Dr. Wright and wish him all the best. I look forward to the day in which he might address these questions. Till then, *oremus pro invicem.*

APPENDIX 2:
TIMELINE OF THE LIFE OF SAINT PAUL

A.D. 8	Birth of Paul[133]
33	Jesus Christ rises from the dead
36	Saul's conversion to Christ on the road to Damascus
36-39	Paul in Arabia & Damascus for three years (Gal 1:18)
39	Paul goes with Barnabas and visits Peter and James in Jerusalem
42-43	James the Greater martyred
	Apostles flee Jerusalem—Peter to Rome
47-48	Paul's First Missionary Journey
49-50	Jerusalem Council, Peter returns from Rome
49/50-52	Paul's Second Missionary Journey
	Paul writes *1&2 Thessalonians*
54/55	Paul writes *Galatians*[134]
56-58	Paul's Third Missionary Journey
57	Paul writes *1 & 2 Corinthians*, *Romans*
58-60	Paul imprisoned in Caesarea
60-61	Paul under house arrest at Rome

	Paul writes *Ephesians, Philippians, Colossians, Philemon*
62	Paul and Luke compose *Hebrews*
63	Luke completes *Acts of the Apostles*
66	Paul authors *1 Timothy* and *Titus*
67	Paul writes *2 Timothy* with the assistance of Luke
	Paul martyred in Rome under Emperor Nero
70	Jerusalem destroyed by Roman legions

Did you benefit from this book?
Please visit amazon.com and leave a review for this book.
Thank you so much! - Taylor

NOTES

[133] The Jubilee Year of Saint Paul that began in 2008 chosen to commemorate the two thousand year anniversary of Saint Paul's birth.

[134] North Galatian Theory: Paul wrote the northern Galatians in 54/55 after his third missionary journey after passing through Galatia and Phrygia mentioned in Acts 18:23.

South Galatian Theory: Paul wrote southern Galatians in 49 after his first missionary journey, probably written from Antioch in Syria.

Appendix 3:
Concordance of Saint Paul's Doctrine

Abortion

✠ Lk 1:41 "the baby leapt in her womb"

✠ Gal 1:15 "he who had set me apart before I was born"

✠ Gal 5:20; Rev 9:2; Rev 21:8 Pharmaceutical abortion condemned. These three passages condemn "sorcery." However, the Greek word used is *pharmakeia*, a word denoting harmful pharmaceutical contraceptives and abortifacients—considered "magical" in ancient civilizations

Baptism of Infants

✠ Acts 2:38-39 "Repent and be baptized... this promise is for you and your children."

✠ Acts 16:15, 16:33, 18:8; 1 Cor 1:16 Household baptisms suggest baptism of children

✠ Rom 6:4 Necessity of baptism

✠ Col 2:11-12 OT circumcision replaced by NT baptism as sign of the covenant (OT circumcision was performed on infants, see Gen 17:12)

Baptismal Regeneration (Born Again)

✠ Acts 2:37-38 "be baptized and receive Holy Spirit"

✠ Acts 22:16 "be baptized and wash away your sins"

✠ Rom 6:4-46 "baptized into death, live in newness of life"
✠ 1 Cor 6:11 "you were *washed*, sanctified, justified"
✠ Titus 3:5 "washing of regeneration"
✠ Heb 10:22 "heart sprinkled, bodies washed in water"

CELIBACY
✠ 1 Cor 7:7-9 – Paul was celibate
✠ 1 Cor 7:32-33 – Paul commends celibacy
✠ 1 Tim 5:9-12 – pledge of celibacy taken by widows

CHURCH AUTHORITY
✠ Acts 2:42 – apostolic doctrine, community & Eucharist
✠ 1 Cor 5:5; 1 Tim 1:20 – Church has power of excommunication
✠ Eph 5:25-26 – Christ loves the Church
✠ 1 Tim 3:15 – Church is "the pillar and foundation of the truth."
✠ Heb 13:17 "obey your leaders and submit to them; for they are keeping watch over your souls"

CHURCH UNITY
✠ Rom 12:4-5 "though many, we are one body in Christ"
✠ Rom 16:17 "avoid those who cause schism"
✠ 1 Cor 1:10 "there should be no divisions among you"
✠ Eph 4:3-6 "one body, one Spirit, one hope, one Lord, on faith, one baptism, one God"

CONFESSION
✠ 2 Cor 5:18 – the Apostles possess the "ministry of reconciliation" to reconcile sinners to God

CONTRACEPTION

✠ 1 Tim 2:11-15 – women saved through childbearing
✠ Gal 5:20; Rev 9:2; Rev 21:8 Artificial means of contraception condemned. These three passages condemn "sorcery." However, the Greek word used is *pharmakeia*, a word denoting harmful pharmaceutical contraceptives and abortifacients— considered "magical" in ancient civilizations

DEUTEROCANONICAL BOOKS ARE SCRIPTURAL

The seven books are: Tobit, Judith, Wisdom, Sirach (Ecclesiasticus), Baruch, and 1 and 2 Maccabees. The Council of Rome in AD 382 formally canonized these seven "deuterocanonical" books along with the rest of the OT and NT as we know it.

Saint Paul refers to and cites these seven deuterocanonical books:
✠ Rom 1:18-32 refers to Wisdom 13:1-9
✠ Heb 11:35 refers to 2 Mac 6:18-7:42

EUCHARIST & REAL PRESENCE

✠ Lk 22:19-20; 1 Cor 10:24-25 "This is my Body…This is my Blood"
✠ 1 Cor 5:7 "Christ our Passover has been sacrificed for us, therefore let us keep the feast" (the Eucharist)
✠ 1 Cor 10:16 eating Eucharist is participation or communion with the Body and Blood of Christ.
✠ 1 Cor 11:26-30 unworthy eating is sinning against the Body and Blood of Christ
✠ Gen 14:18; Heb 7:1-17 - Christ is a priest like Melchizedek, offering bread and wine
✠ Acts 2:42 "breaking of bread" refers to Eucharist

✠ Heb 13:10 Christian worship involves an "altar"

FAITH & WORKS
✠ Gal 5:6 "faith working in love"
✠ Phil 2:12; 2 Cor 5:10; Rom 2:6-10, 13, 3:31; Mt 25:32-46; Gal 6:6-10 works have merit

HOMOSEXUALITY
✠ Rom 1:27 Homosexuality called unnatural, shameful, and a perversity
✠ 1 Cor 6:9 Active homosexuals will not inherit the kingdom of God
✠ 1 Tim 1:9-10 Homosexuals called "sinners"

MARY
✠ Lk 1:28 "Hail, *full of grace*! The Lord is with you." The Greek word for "full of grace" is *kecharitomene*, denoting a plenitude of grace. Wherever grace is full, sin is absent.
✠ Lk 1:42-48 "blessed are you among women"
✠ Lk 1:43 Mary is "Mother of God"

ORIGINAL SIN
✠ Rom 5:12-19 Many became sinners through one man's sin
✠ 1 Cor 15:21-23 "by man came death; in Adam all die"

PRIESTHOOD
✠ Rom 15:16 Paul is "a minister of Christ Jesus with the *priestly duty* of proclaiming the gospel of God"
✠ Acts 1:15-26; 2 Tim 2:2; Tit 1:5 An unbroken Apostolic Succession of laying on of hands

✠ Acts 15:6, 23; 1 Tim 4:14, 5:22; 1 Tim 5:17
Presbyters/elders (priests) were ordained to preach
and administer the sacraments.

✠ Lk 16:24; Rom 4; 1 Cor 4:14-15; Acts 7:2; 1 Thess
2:11; 1 Jn 2:13-14 Ministers called "father"

✠ Gen 14:18; Ps 110:4; Heb 7:1-17 Christ is priest
forever according to order of Melchizedek, offering
bread and wine.

PURGATORY & PRAYERS FOR THE DEAD

✠ 1 Cor 3:15 "he himself will be saved, but only as one
escaping through the flames."

✠ Lk 12:59 example of temporal punishment

✠ Col 1:24 "extra" suffering

✠ 2 Tim 1:15-18 Paul prays for the now deceased
Onesiphorus for "that Day"

✠ Heb 12:6-11 God's painful discipline

✠ Heb 12:23 Souls in heaven "having been made
perfect."

RELICS

✠ Acts 19:11,12 Handkerchiefs and aprons touched to
Paul's body heal the sick (3rd class relic)

✠ Acts 5:15-16 Peter's shadow thought to heal the sick

SAINTS

✠ 1 Cor 12:25-27; Rom 12:4-5 Saint make up the body
of Christ

✠ Eph 6:18; Rom 15:30; Col 4:3; 1 Thess 1:11
Intercessory prayer for one another

✠ 1 Cor 13:12 Saints also united with God

SALVATION
Past Event
"I have been saved"

✠ Rom 8:24 "in this hope you were saved"
✠ Eph 2:5-8 "by grace you have been saved"
✠ 2 Tim 1:9 "He saved us, He called us"
✠ Titus 3:5 "He saved us though the washing of regeneration"

Present Process
"I am being saved"
✠ Phil 2:12 "work out your salvation with fear and trembling"

Future Event
"I will be saved"
✠ Acts 15:11 "we shall be saved through the grace of Jesus"
✠ Rom 5:9-10 "since we are justified, we shall be saved"
✠ Rom 13:11 "salvation is nearer now than when we first believed"
✠ 1 Cor 3:15 "he will be saved, but only through fire"
✠ Heb 9:28 Jesus will appear again to bring salvation

"ONCE SAVED ALWAYS SAVED" DENIED BY SCRIPTURE
✠ Rom 11:21-22 Spare branches, continue or be cut off.
✠ 1 Cor 9:27 "I beat my body and make it my slave so that after I have preached to others, I myself will not be disqualified for the prize."
✠ 1 Cor 10:12 "So, if you think you are standing firm, be careful that you don't fall!."
✠ Gal 5:4 "you have fallen from grace"
✠ Phil 2:12 "work out salvation with fear and trembling."

✠ Heb 4:1 "the promise of entering his rest still stands, let us be careful that none of you be found to have fallen short of it."

✠ Heb 6:4-6 Describes "enlightened" Christians who have fallen away from Christ

✠ Heb 10:26-29 "worse punishment ... for the man who has spurned the Son of God, and profaned the blood of the covenant by which he was sanctified, and outraged the Spirit of grace"

SCRIPTURE & TRADITION

✠ 2 Thess 2:15; 2 Tim 2:2; 1 Cor 11:2; 1 Thess 2:13 - Paul speaks of oral tradition

✠ Acts 2:42 Early Christians followed apostolic tradition

✠ Acts 8:31; Heb 5:12 Guidance needed to interpret Scriptures

✠ 2 Tim 3:16 "All scripture, inspired of God, is profitable to teach, to reprove, to correct, to instruct in justice"

SEVEN SACRAMENTS OF CHRIST

✠ Baptism – Rom 6:4-6

✠ Confirmation – Acts 8:14-17; Heb 6:2

✠ Eucharist – 1 Cor 10:24-25

✠ Penance – 2 Cor 5:18

✠ Extreme Unction – Mk 6:13; James 5:14-15

✠ Holy Orders – Acts 6:3-6; 1 Tim. 3:1-9; 4:14-16; 5:17-19-22

✠ Matrimony – Eph 5:31-32

BIBLIOGRAPHY

Alexander Roberts, James Donaldson and A. Cleveland Coxe. *The Ante-Nicene Fathers Vols. 1-10: Translations of the Writings of the Fathers Down to A.D. 325.* Harbor: Logos Research Systems, 1997).

Aquinas, Thomas. *Summa Theologica.* Translated by Fathers of the English Dominican Province. Notre Dame, IN: Christian Classics, Ave Maria Press, 1981 [1948].

Barber, Michael. *Singing in the Reign: The Psalms and the Liturgy of God's Kingdom.* Steubenville, Ohio: Emmaus Road Publishing, 2001.

Bassler, Jouette M. *Navigating Paul: An Introduction to Key Theological Concepts.* Westminster John Knox Press, 2006.

Biblia Hebraica Stuttgartensia. K. Elliger and W. Rudolph, eds. Stuttgart: Deutche Bibelgesellschaft, Fourth Corrected Edition, 1990.

Biblia Sacra Juxta Vulgatam Clementinam. Bellingham, WA: Logos Research Systems, 2005.

Bird, Michael F. *A Bird's Eye View of Paul.* Inter-Varsity Press, 2008.

_____. *The Saving Righteousness of God: Studies on Paul, Justification and the New Perspective.* Wipf & Stock Publishers, 2007.

Boyarin, Daniel. *A Radical Jew: Paul and the Politics of Identity* (University of California Press), 1994.

Brondos, David A. *Paul on the Cross: Reconstructing the Apostle's Story of Redemption.* Fortress Press, 2006.

Brown, Peter. *The Cult of the Saints: Its Rise and Function in Latin Christianity.* Chicago: University of Chicago Press, 1981.

Bruce, F.F. 'Is the Paul of Acts the Real Paul?' Bulletin *John Rylands Library* 58 (1976) 283–305.

Calvin, John. *Institutes of the Christian Religion.* 2 Vols. Translated by Ford Lewis Battles. John T. McNeill, ed. Westminster John Knox, 2006.

Campbell, Douglas A. *The Quest for Paul's Gospel: A Suggested Strategy.* London: T&T Clark, 2005.

Campbell, William S. *Paul and the Creation of Christian Identity.* London: T&T Clark, 2008.

Carson, D.A. O'Brien, Peter T., and Seifrid, Mark, eds., *Justification and Variegated Nomism: The Paradoxes of Paul.* Grand Rapids, MI: Baker Book House, 2004.

Catechism of the Catholic Church. Second ed. Vatican City: Libreria Editrice Vaticana, 1997.

Catechism of Trent. New York: Baronius Press, 2019.

Chesterton, G.K. *Orthodoxy.* Wheaton, Illinois: Harold Shaw Publishers, 1994.

Chronicles – Maccabees: The Navarre Bible Commentary. Jose Maria Casciaro, ed. New York: Scepter Publishers, 2003.

Cochini, Christian. *The Apostolic Origins of Priestly Celibacy.* Trans. Nelly Marans. San Francisco: Ignatius Press, 1990.

Codex Iuris Canonici. Vatican City: Libreria Editrice Vaticana, 1983.

Creeds of Christendom: With a History and Critical Notes, Volume 1. Philip Schaff and David S. Schaff, eds. Grand Rapids: Baker Books, 1998.

Danielou, Jean. *The Bible and Liturgy.* Notre Dame, IN: University of Notre Dame Press, 1956.

Dix, Dom Gregory. *The Shape of the Liturgy.* New York: Seabury, 1982.

Dunn, James D.G. and Suggate, Alan M. *The Justice of God: A Fresh Look at the Old Doctrine of Justification by Faith.* Grand Rapids, MI: Wm. B. Eerdmans, 1993.

Dunn, James D.G. ed. *Paul and the Mosaic Law.* Grand Rapids, MI: Wm. B. Eerdmans, 2001.

_____. *The Cambridge Companion to St Paul.* Cambridge University Press, 2003.

_____. *Epistle to the Galatians.* Peabody, Massachusetts: Hendrickson Publishers, 1995.

_____. *Jesus, Paul and the Law.* Louisville, KY: Westminster John Knox Press, 1990.

_____. *Jesus, Paul, and the Law: Studies in Mark and Galatians.* Westminster-John Knox Press, 1990.

_____. *The New Perspective on Paul: Revised Edition.* Grand Rapids, MI: Wm. B. Eerdmans, 2007.

_____. *The Theology of Paul the Apostle* Grand Rapids, MI: Wm. B. Eerdmans, 1997.

_____. *The Theology of Paul's Letter to the Galatians.* Cambridge University Press, 1993.

_____. *Word Biblical Commentary, Romans 1-8.* Dallas, TX: Word Books, 1988.

Eisenbaum, Pamela. *Paul Was Not a Christian: The Original Message of a Misunderstood Apostle.* Harper One, 2009.

Gager, John G. *Reinventing Paul.* Oxford University Press, 2000.

Gorman, Michael J. *Apostle of the Crucified Lord: A Theological Introduction to Paul and His Letters.* Grand Rapids, MI: Wm. B. Eerdmans, 2004.

Greek New Testament: Fourth Revised Edition. Kurt Aland, Matthew Black, Carlo M. Martini et al. Deutsche Bibelgesellschaft, 1993; 2006.

Hahn, Scott. *Kinship by Covenant*. New Haven: Yale University Press, 2009.

_____. *Letter and Spirit: From Written Text to Living Word in the Liturgy*. New York: Doubleday, 2005.

_____. *The Lamb's Supper: The Mass as Heaven on Earth*. New York: Doubleday, 1999.

Horsley, Richard A. and Silberman, Neil Asher. *The Message and the Kingdom: How Jesus and Paul Ignited a Revolution and Transformed the Ancient World*. Augsburg Fortress Publishers, 2002.

_____. *Paul and Empire: Religion and Power in Roman Imperial Society*. Trinity Press International, 1997.

Husbands, Mark, and Treier, Daniel J., ed. *Justification: What's at Stake in the Current Debates*. InterVarsity Press, 2004.

Jordan, James. *Through New Eyes: Developing a Biblical View of the World*. Eugene, Oregon: Wipf & Stock Publishers, 2000.

Josephus, Flavius. *Jewish Antiquities: Books I-III*. Loeb Classical Library No. 242. Trans. H. St. John Thackeray. Cambridge, MA: Harvard University Press, 1997.

_____. *The Works of Josephus: New Updated Edition*. Trans. William Whiston. Peabody, MA: Hendrickson Publishers, 1987.

Kaylor, R. David. *Paul's Covenant Community: Jew & Gentile in Romans*. Atlanta, GA: John Knox Press, 1989.

Kim, Seyoon. *Christ and Caesar: The Gospel and the Roman Empire in the Writings of Paul and Luke*. Grand Rapids, MI: Wm. B. Eerdmans, 2008.

_____. *Paul and the New Perspective: Second Thoughts on the Origin of Paul's Gospel*. Grand Rapids, MI: Wm. B. Eerdmans, 2001.

Kline, Meredith. *Treaty of the Great King*. Grand Rapids, MI: William B. Eerdmans Publishing, 1963.

Leithart, Peter. *The Kingdom and the Power*. Phillipsburg, NJ: Presbyterian and Reformed Publishing, 1993.

Levering, Matthew. *Christ's Fulfillment of Torah and Temple: Salvation according to Thomas Aquinas*. Notre Dame, Indiana: University of Notre Dame Press, 2002.

Luther, Martin. *Luther's Works*. Vols. 1-30. Edited and Translated by Jaroslav Peliakn, et al. Saint Louis: Concordia Publishing House. Vols. 31-55. Philadelphia: Fortress Press, 1955-1979.

LXX Septuaginta. Alfred Ralfs, ed. Stuttgart: Wurttembergische Bebelanstalt/Deutsche Bibelgesellschaft, 1935.

Maimonides. *Mishneh Torah: The Book of Knowledge*. Translated by Moses Hyamson. New York: Bloch, 1938.

McGrath, Alister E. Ius*titia Dei: A History of the Christian Doctrine of Justification*. Third Edition. Cambridge University Press, 2005.

Meech, John. *Paul in Israel's Story: Self and Community at the Cross*. Oxford University Press, 2006.

Missale Romanum. Editio Typica Tertia. Vatican: Typus Vaticanis, 2002.

Murphy-O'Connor, Jerome. *Jesus and Paul: Parallel Lives*. Collegeville, Minn.: Liturgical Press, 2007.

_____. *Paul the Letter-Writer: His World, His Options, His Skills*. Collegeville, Minn.: Liturgical Press, 1995.

_____. *Paul: A Critical Life*. Oxford: Clarendon Press, 1996.

Nanos, Mark D. ed., *The Galatians Debate: Contemporary Issues in Rhetorical and Historical Interpretation*. Hendrickson Publishers, 2002.

_____. *The Irony of Galatians: Paul's Letter in First-Century Context*. Augsburg Fortress, 2001.

_____. *The Mystery of Romans: The Jewish Context of Paul's Letter.* Fortress Press, 1996.

Neusner, Jacob. *A Rabbi Talks with Jesus.* New York: Doubleday, 1993.

Ott, Ludwig, *Fundamentals of Catholic Dogma.* Charlotte, North Carolina: TAN Books, 1974.

Oxford Dictionary of the Christian Church. F. L. Cross, ed. New York: Oxford University Press, 1997.

Pate, Marvin C. *The Reverse of the Curse: Paul, Wisdom, and the Law.* Coronet Books, 2001.

Pelikan, Jaroslav. *The Emergence of the Catholic Tradition (100-600).* Chicago: University of Chicago Press, 1971.

Philip. Schaff. *The Nicene and Post-Nicene Fathers* Vol. 1-14. Oak Harbor: Logos Research Systems, 1997.

Philo Judaeus. *The Works of Philo: Complete and Unabridged, New Updated Edition.* Trans. C. D. Yonge. Peabody, Massachusetts: Hendrickson Publishers, 1993.

Pitre, Brant. *Jesus, the Tribulation, and the End of the Exile.* Grand Rapids: Baker Academic, 2006.

Rapa, Robert Keith. *The Meaning of 'Works of the Law' in Galatians and Romans.* New York: Peter Lang, 2001.

Ratzinger, Joseph. *God is Near Us: The Eucharist, the Heart of Life.* San Francisco: Ignatius Press, 2003.

_____. *Jesus of Nazareth.* New York: Doubleday, 2007.

Rosini, Ruggero. *Mariology of Blessed John Duns Scotus.* Trans. Peter M. Fehlner. New Bedford, Massachusetts: Academy of the Immaculate, 2008.

Ruef, John. *Paul's First letter to Corinth.* New York: Penguin, 1971.

Sanders, E.P. *Paul and Palestinian Judaism: A Comparison of Patterns of Religion.* Minneapolis, MN: Fortress Press, 1977.

_____. *Paul, the Law, and the Jewish People*. Minneapolis, MN: Fortress Press, 1983.

Schreiner, Thomas R. *The Law & Its Fulfillment: A Pauline Theology of Law*. Grand Rapids, MI: Baker Book House, 1993.

Segal, Alan F. *Paul, the Convert*. New Haven: Yale University Press, 1990.

Stendahl, Krister. *Paul Among Jews and Gentiles and Other Essays*. Philadelphia, PA: Fortress Press, 1976.

Stuhlmacher, Peter and Hagner, Donald Alfred. *Revisiting Paul's Doctrine of Justification: A Challenge to the New Perspective*. Intervarsity Press, 2001.

Tekeyan, V. "La Mère de Dieu dans la liturgie armenienne," in Maria. Etudes surla Sainte Vierge, ed. H. du Manoir, S.J., v. 1, Paris, 1949.

Holy Bible: Revised Standard Version Catholic Edition. Catholic Biblical Association, 1997.

Thielman, Frank. *Paul and the Law: A Contextual Approach*. Downers Grove, IL: InterVarsity Press, 1994.

Thompson, Michael B. *The New Perspective on Paul*. Cambridge: Grove Books Limited, 2002.

Thurian, Max. *The Eucharistic Memorial*. Richmond, VA: John Knox Press, 1962.

Vatican Council II: The Basic Sixteen Documents. Flannery, Austen, ed. Northport, New York: Costello Publishing Company, 1996.

Vos, Gerhardus. *Biblical Theology: Old and New Testaments*. Carlisle, Pennsylvania: Banner of Truth Trust, 1996.

Waters, G.P. *Justification and the New Perspectives on Paul: A Review and Response*. P&R Publishing, 2004.

Watson, Francis. *Paul, Judaism, and the Gentiles: Beyond the New Perspective*. Grand Rapids, Michigan: Wm. B. Eerdmans Pub. Co., 2007.

Watts, Rikki E. "On the Edge of the Millennium: Making Sense of Genesis 1" in *Living in the Lamblight: Christianity and Contemporary Challenges to the Gospel.* Vancouver: Regent College Publications, 2001: 129-151.

Weingreen, J. *A Practical Grammar for Classical Hebrew.* New York: Oxford University Press, 1959.

Westerholm, Stephen. *Israel's Law and the Church's Faith: Paul and His Recent Interpreters.* Wipf & Stock Publishers, 1998.

Williams, D.S. "Reconsidering Marcion's Gospel," *Journal of Biblical Literature* 108 (1989): 477-96.

Wright, N. T. *Climax of the Covenant.* Minneapolis: Augsburg Fortress Publishers, 1993.

_____. *Jesus and the Victory of God.* Minneapolis: Fortress Press, 1996.

_____. *Justification: God's Plan and Paul's Vision.* London: SPCK, 2009.

_____. *Paul: Fresh Perspective.* Fortress Press, 2005.

_____. *The New Testament and the People of God.* Minneapolis: Fortress Press, 1992.

_____. *The Resurrection of the Son of God.* Minneapolis: Augsburg Fortress Publishers, 2003.

_____. *What Saint Paul Really Said: Was Paul of Tarsus the Real Founder of Christianity?* Wm. B. Eerdmans, 1997.

Yinger, Kent L. *Paul, Judaism, and Judgment According to Deeds.* Cambridge University Press, 1999.

Young, Brad H. Paul the Jewish Theologian: A Pharisee among Christians, Jews, and Gentiles. Peabody, Massachusetts: Hendrickson Publishers, 1998.

INDEX

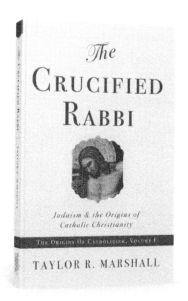

THE CRUCIFIED RABBI
Origins of Catholicism, Volume 1

TAYLOR MARSHALL'S NEXT BOOK...

THE ETERNAL CITY:
ROME AND THE ORIGINS OF CATHOLIC CHRISTIANITY
Origins of Catholicism, Volume 3

An exposition of how Christ and the Apostles intended the Church to move its capital from Jerusalem to Rome, based on the prophecies of Daniel. Never before has there been a theological and historical examination of the prerogatives of the city of Rome in Christ's plan for human redemption.

ABOUT TAYLOR MARSHALL

Taylor and his wife Joy live in Dallas, Texas with their eight children. Taylor holds a Ph.D. in Philosophy from the University of Dallas focusing on the Natural Law theory of Saint Thomas Aquinas. He is a graduate of Texas A&M University (BA, Philosophy) Westminster Theological Seminary (MAR, Systematic Theology), Nashotah Theological House (Certificate in Anglican Studies), and the University of Dallas (MA, Philosophy). He is the best-selling author of nine books, including *Infiltration* and *Sword and Serpent*. Learn more at

TaylorMarshall.com

Made in the USA
Coppell, TX
15 December 2021

68643027R00156